# English through the News Media

## —2023 Edition—


Masami Takahashi

Noriko Itoh

Richard Powe


JN089203

Asahi Press

記事提供
The New York Times
New York Post
The Japan Times
The Guardian
Forbes
AFP-JIJI

写真提供
アフロ：The New York Times／Redux／
ロイター／AP／WESTEND61
AFP／WAA
イメージマート

地図・イラスト
ヨシオカユリ

*English through the News Media —2023 Edition—*
Copyright © 2023 by Asahi Press

All rights reserved. No part of this book may be reproduced or transmitted in any form or by any means, electronic or mechanical, including photocopying, recording or by any information storage and retrieval system, without permission in writing from authors and the publisher.

# はしがき

本書は、世界のニュースを通して Reading, Listening, Speaking, Writing のバランスのとれた学習が効果的にできるように工夫してあります。2021年10月：人類と気候変動との関わりに対する研究でノーベル物理学賞、11月：大谷翔平選手　ア・リーグMVPに誰もが納得；超金持ちでも相続時に悲惨な目に；仕事の未来：流行りの職場５選、12月：スリランカ　有機農法を始めて大惨事に；ニカラグアが台湾との同盟破棄；マッチング・アプリで実際のデートは？、2022年１月：アフリカでクーデター多発の理由、２月：平野歩夢　北京五輪での金メダル・ストーリー；日本の労働組合は男性中心、女性指導者の誕生で変わるのか；五輪選手　米中間の対抗意識に巻き込まれる；カナダでトラック運転手が抗議活動　何故？；中国との争いで小国のリトアニア・ブランドが排斥される；トンガ　自然の猛威被害が３度目；気候変動は人類の順応より早く地球をダメにする、３月：韓国での「多文化主義」とは；ビゴレクシア（筋肉醜形恐怖症）とは；アブラモヴィッチの資産凍結でチェルシーが危機状態に；民族主義と帝国主義に基づくプーチンのウクライナ戦争；中国　離婚率と結婚率低下；日本映画『ドライブ・マイカー』が米アカデミー賞受賞、４月：ベンガル湾で大洪水　住民はマングローブの森に避難；シンガポール　「不当感」の増大で死刑反対意見強まる；リオのカーニバルのパレードを巡り争い騒ぎ；トルコで超インフレとの戦い；空飛ぶバッテリーでジェット燃料不要；ロシア人　プーチン政権から逃れ、ウクライナ避難民と共にイスラエルに；不平等が野放しの富裕国の国民は不幸になる；大谷翔平選手　「神懸かりな」歴史的夜；マクロン大統領　ルペンに競り勝ち再選し仏統一を誓う、まで世界中のニュースを満載しております。

*The New York Times, The Japan Times, The Guardian, New York Post, Forbes* から社会・文化・政治経済・情報・言語・教育・科学・医学・環境・娯楽・スポーツなどのあらゆる分野を網羅しましたので、身近に世界中のニュースに触れ、読み、聞き、話し、書く楽しさを育みながら、多角的にそして複眼的に英語運用力が自然に培われるように意図しています。

26課より構成され、各課に新聞記事読解前にBefore you readを設けました。本文の内容が予想できる写真と、どこにあるかを示す地図と国の情報を参照しながら自由に意見交換をします。次の Words and Phrases では、記事に記載されている単語や熟語とそれに合致する英語の説明を選び、あらかじめ大事な語の理解を深めて行きます。Summaryでは記事の内容を予想しながら、５語を適当な箇所に記入して要約文を完成させます。記事読解前では難しいようであれば、読解後に活用しても良いと思います。さらに、記事に関連した裏話も載せました。記事の読解にあたり、わかり易い註釈を記事の右端に付け、理解度をチェックするための Multiple Choice, True or False, 記事に関連した語法を学ぶVocabularyと豊富に取り揃えました。Summaryと記事がそのまま音声化されたファイルをウェブ上にあげています。多方面に渡る記事やExercisesを活用して、英字新聞に慣れ親しみ、使っていただけることを望んでいます。

今回テキスト作成に際して、お世話になりました朝日出版社社長原雅久氏、編集部の日比野忠氏、小川洋一郎氏に心からお礼申し上げます。

2022年10月

高橋　優身
伊藤　典子
Richard Powell

## CONTENTS

＊印の15章を *15 Selected Units of English Through the News Media —2023 Edition—*として別途刊行しています。

# English through the News Media 2023 Edition

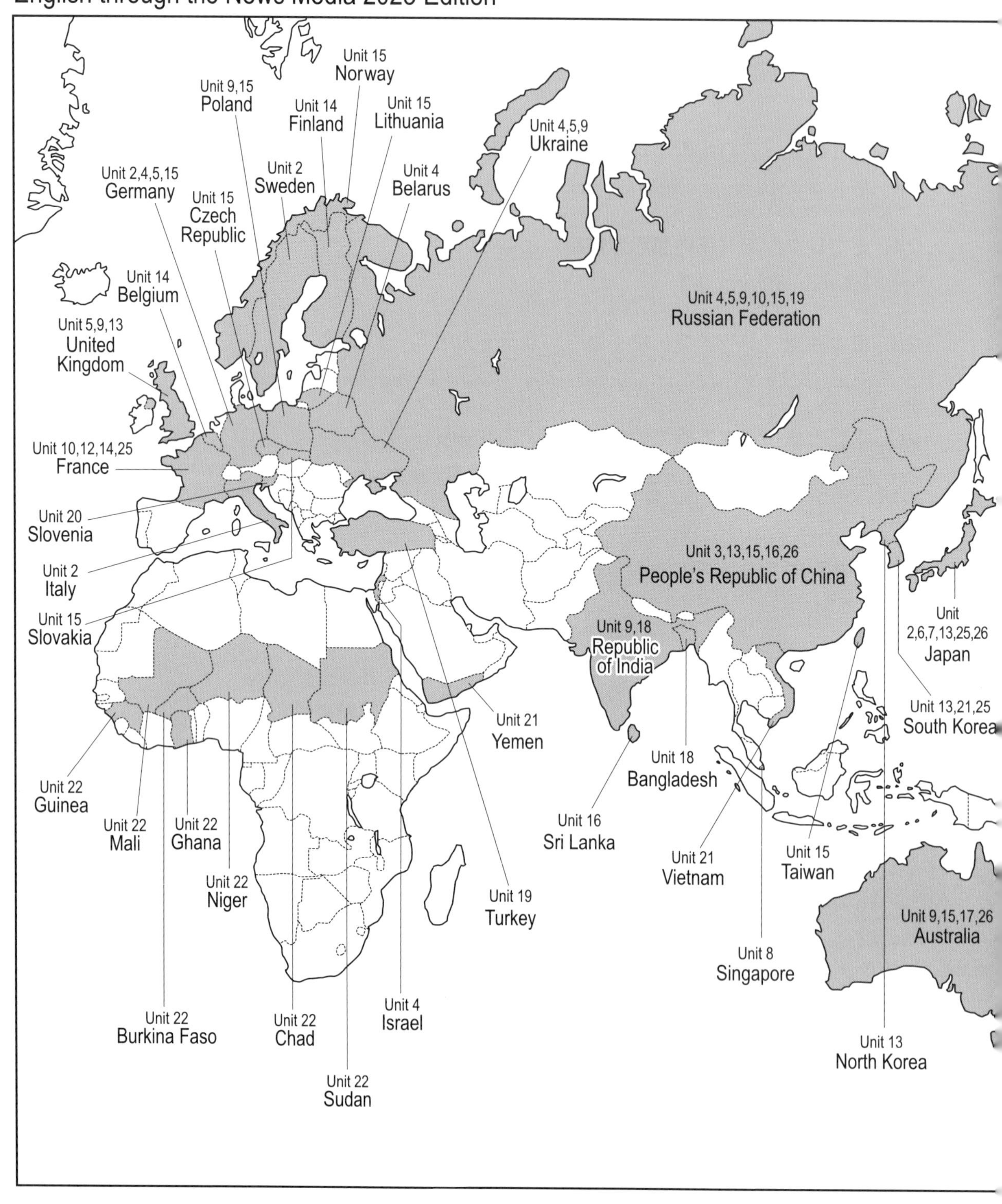

Unit 15
Norway
Unit 9,15
Poland
Unit 14
Finland
Unit 15
Lithuania
Unit 4,5,9
Ukraine
Unit 2,4,5,15
Germany
Unit 2
Sweden
Unit 4
Belarus
Unit 15
Czech
Republic
Unit 14
Belgium
Unit 5,9,13
United
Kingdom
Unit 4,5,9,10,15,19
Russian Federation
Unit 10,12,14,25
France
Unit 20
Slovenia
Unit 2
Italy
Unit 3,13,15,16,26
People's Republic of China
Unit 15
Slovakia
Unit 9,18
Republic
of India
Unit
2,6,7,13,25,26
Japan
Unit 21
Yemen
Unit 13,21,25
South Korea
Unit 18
Bangladesh
Unit 22
Guinea
Unit 22
Mali
Unit 22
Ghana
Unit 16
Sri Lanka
Unit 21
Vietnam
Unit 15
Taiwan
Unit 22
Niger
Unit 19
Turkey
Unit 9,15,17,26
Australia
Unit 8
Singapore
Unit 4
Israel
Unit 22
Burkina Faso
Unit 22
Chad
Unit 13
North Korea
Unit 22
Sudan

Unit 6,14,22
Canada
Unit 1,2,3,4,6,9,15,16,20,24,25,26
U.S.A.
Unit 9
Mexico
Unit 15
Nicaragua
Unit 23
Brazil
Unit 9
Peru
Unit 17
Tonga
Unit 14
New Zealand

## 音声再生アプリ「リスニング・トレーナー」を使った音声ダウンロード

朝日出版社開発のアプリ、「リスニング・トレーナー(リストレ)」を使えば、教科書の音声をスマホ、タブレットに簡単にダウンロードできます。どうぞご活用ください。

### ◉ アプリ【リスニング・トレーナー】の使い方

**《アプリのダウンロード》**

App StoreまたはGoogle Playから「リスニング・トレーナー」のアプリ(無料)をダウンロード

App Storeはこちら▶

Google Playはこちら▶

**《アプリの使い方》**

① アプリを開き「コンテンツを追加」をタップ

② 画面上部に**【15696】**を入力しDoneをタップ

## 音声ストリーミング配信 〉〉〉

この教科書の音声は、右記ウェブサイトにて無料で配信しています。

https://text.asahipress.com/free/english/

# English through the News Media

Unit **1**

# ●気候変動は人類の順応より早く地球をダメにする

フィリピン・マニラ首都圏の低地に沿う護岸。これで高潮から住民を守れるのか？大丈夫？

The New York Times ／ Redux ／アフロ

## ***Before you read***

### Questions

**1.** What do you think the article will be about?

この記事は何の話題についてだと思いますか？

**2.** Do you think it is already too late to stop global warming?

地球温暖化を止めるにはもう手遅れだと思いますか？

## Words and Phrases

次の１～５の語の説明として最も近いものをａ～ｅから１つ選び、(　　) 内に記入しなさい。

**1.** convene (　　)
**2.** unleash (　　)
**3.** damning (　　)
**4.** scarcity (　　)
**5.** irreversible (　　)

**a.** shortage
**b.** release something dangerous
**c.** impossible to heal or restore
**d.** assemble for a meeting
**e.** blameworthy

## Summary

次の英文は記事の要約です。下の語群から最も適切な語を１つ選び、(　　) 内に記入しなさい。

1-02

A new report commissioned by the U.N. (　　　) that we are not taking global warming seriously. More and more people are being (　　　) by floods, droughts, extreme heat or crop failures. Although some countries have taken temporary (　　　) they are not nearly enough. (　　　) we cut fossil fuel consumption global warming will (　　　) get worse.

affected　　concludes　　measures　　only　　unless

国連の気候変動に関する政府間パネル（IPCC）による第６次評価報告書が、2021年８月から2022年４月にかけて順次公表された。22年４月現在、気温はすでに1.1度上昇しているが、1.5度以下に抑えるという目標のため、2025年までに二酸化炭素（$CO_2$）などの温室効果ガス排出量を減少させ、$CO_2$の回収や貯蔵を進める必要があると訴えている。対策として、発電分野では化石燃料から温室効果ガスを出さない再生可能エネルギーへの転換をはかり、電気自動車（EV）の導入、建物の断熱化やテレワークを進める。

また、再生エネルギーの太陽光発電とリチウムイオン電池は85％、風力発電は55％のコスト削減があり導入し易くなった。日本は、温室効果ガス排出量について「2030年度に46％減」「50年に実質ゼロ」の目標を掲げている。気候市民会議の取り組みが欧州で始められて以来、日本でも色々な立場の市民の意見を反映させ、地球温暖化問題を「自分事」として捉えてもらおうと取り組みが行われている。

ところが、2022年２月ロシアのウクライナ侵攻で、世界のエネルギー事情は一変した。ロシアに経済制裁を課しているため、ロシアからのエネルギーに依存していた欧州各国は、温室効果ガスを出す石炭火力など、使えるものは何でも使っている。原油価格や天然ガス価格が最高値を示している。日本はエネルギー自給率が11％しかなく、ロシアへの経済制裁前は、天然ガスの９％、石油の４％をロシアから輸入していた。気候変動対策とエネルギー安全保障を両立させるためには、再生可能エネルギーの利用拡大、省エネの推進、原子力発電の活用を考えなければならない。

## Reading

1-03

# Climate Change Is Harming the Planet Faster Than We Can Adapt, U.N. Warns

Countries aren't doing nearly enough to protect against the disasters to come as the planet keeps heating up, a major new scientific report concludes.

The dangers of climate change are mounting so rapidly that they could soon overwhelm the ability of both nature and humanity to adapt unless greenhouse gas emissions are quickly reduced, according to a major new scientific report released on Monday.

1-04

The report by the Intergovernmental Panel on Climate Change, a body of experts convened by the United Nations, is the most detailed look yet at the threats posed by global warming. It concludes that nations aren't doing nearly enough to protect cities, farms and coastlines from the hazards that climate change has unleashed so far, such as record droughts and rising seas, let alone from the even greater disasters in store as the planet continues to warm.

Written by 270 researchers from 67 countries, the report is "an atlas of human suffering and a damning indictment of failed climate leadership," said António Guterres, the United Nations secretary general.

1-05

In 2019, storms, floods and other extreme weather events displaced more than 13 million people across Asia and Africa. Rising heat and drought are killing crops and trees, putting millions worldwide at increased risk of hunger and malnutrition, while mosquitoes carrying diseases like malaria and dengue are spreading into new areas. Roughly half the world's population currently faces severe water scarcity at least part of the year.

To date, many nations have been able to partly limit the damage by spending billions of dollars each year on adaptation measures like flood barriers, air-conditioning or

- to come：来たるべき《未来を示し、直前の名詞を修飾》
- overwhelm ～：～を圧倒する
- greenhouse gas emission：温室効果ガス排出
- reduced：削減される
- body：集まり
- convened：召集された
- look at ～：～についての考察
- posed：もたらされた
- let alone ～：～はもちろん、言うまでもなく
- in store：差し迫る
- indictment of ～：～に対する起訴
- failed climate leadership：気候変動に関してリーダーシップが発揮できなかったこと
- secretary general：事務総長
- extreme weather events：異常気象
- malnutrition：栄養失調
- dengue：デング熱
- water scarcity：水不足
- To date：今日まで
- flood barriers：防潮堤

early-warning systems for tropical cyclones.

1-06

But those efforts are too often "incremental," the report said. Preparing for future threats, like dwindling freshwater supplies or irreversible ecosystem damage, will require "transformational" changes that involve rethinking how people build homes, grow food, produce energy and protect nature.

- tropical cyclones：熱帯低気圧
- "incremental"：「漸進的な」
- dwindling：減少する
- irreversible：不可逆的な
- "transformational"：「変革的な」

The report also carries a stark warning: If temperatures keep rising, many parts of the world could soon face limits in how much they can adapt to a changing environment. If nations don't act quickly to slash fossil fuel emissions and halt global warming, more and more people will suffer unavoidable loss or be forced to flee their homes, creating dislocation on a global scale.

- stark：厳しい
- slash ～：～を削減する
- fossil fuel：化石燃料
- dislocation：混乱

1-07

If average warming passes 1.5 degrees Celsius, even humanity's best efforts to adapt could falter, the report warns. The cost of defending coastal communities against rising seas could exceed what many nations can afford. In some regions, including parts of North America, livestock and outdoor workers could face rising levels of heat stress that make farming increasingly difficult, said Rachel Bezner Kerr, an agricultural expert at Cornell University who contributed to the report.

- Celsius：摂氏
- falter：衰える、弱体化する

Poor nations are far more exposed to climate risks than rich countries. Between 2010 and 2020, droughts, floods and storms killed 15 times as many people in highly vulnerable countries, including those in Africa and Asia, as in the wealthiest countries, the report said.

- 15 times：15倍
- vulnerable：脆弱な

by Brad Plummer and Raymond Zhong
*The New York Times, February 28, 2022*

## Exercises

### Multiple Choice

次の１～５の英文を完成させるために、ａ～ｄの中から最も適切なものを１つ選びなさい。

1. The writer warns that rising greenhouse gas emissions may
   - **a.** harm consumer protection.
   - **b.** bring worldwide crises.
   - **c.** increase the cutting of trees.
   - **d.** see the beginning of global warming.

2. ______________________________ unless the earth can be cooled.
   - **a.** Overwhelming disasters such as floods will strike
   - **b.** More air disasters such as plane crashes will be reported
   - **c.** Terrible disasters such as earthquakes will happen
   - **d.** Financial disasters such as bankruptcies will result

3. Many wealthy nations have been able to restrict the damage by
   - **a.** voting out unpopular governments.
   - **b.** giving help to wealthier citizens.
   - **c.** spending a huge amount of money on flood protection.
   - **d.** increasing the supply of electricity.

4. Rising temperatures and droughts are
   - **a.** halting global emissions.
   - **b.** harming food production.
   - **c.** heating fossil fuels.
   - **d.** humbling politicians.

5. According to the report, measures to deal with the crisis have been
   - **a.** non-existent.
   - **b.** limited and inadequate.
   - **c.** overly ambitious.
   - **d.** irreversible.

## True or False

本文の内容に合致するものにT (True)、合致しないものにF (False) をつけなさい。

( ) **1.** If rising heat kills trees and crops, millions of people will get malnourished.

( ) **2.** One crucial goal is to keep temperature rises under 1.5 degrees.

( ) **3.** "Transformational" change means rethinking how to produce energy and protect nature.

( ) **4.** Rich countries suffer fewer climate risks than poor countries.

( ) **5.** Due to global warming, mosquitos are carrying diseases like smallpox and coronavirus.

## Vocabulary

次の1～8は、「climate change 気候変動」に関する英文です。日本文に合わせて( )内に最も適切な語を下の語群から1つ選び、記入しなさい。

**1.** 気候変動問題は、緊急の注意を向ける必要がある。
The ( ) issue requires urgent attention.

**2.** 地球温暖化は、人類の脅威である。
( ) is a threat to mankind.

**3.** 水力発電は、温室効果ガスの排出量が極めて小さい。
Hydropower emits almost no ( ) gases.

**4.** 天然ガスは、化石燃料だ。
Natural gas is a ( ).

**5.** 我々は、二酸化炭素を削減する必要がある。
We need to reduce ( ).

**6.** 干ばつは、食料不足を招いた。
The ( ) led to an insufficiency of food.

**7.** 大雨で道路が冠水した。
Heavy rains have ( ) the road.

**8.** 50万人以上の子供たちが、いまだに栄養失調に苦しんでいる。
More than half a million children still suffer from ( ).

| carbon dioxide | climate change | drought | flooded |
|---|---|---|---|
| fossil fuel | global warming | greenhouse | malnutrition |

Unit 2

# 人類と気候変動との関わりに対する研究でノーベル物理学賞

「人類と気候変動との関わり」で2021年ノーベル物理学賞を受賞した
眞鍋淑郎博士　AFP／WAA

## Before you read

Kingdom of Sweden
スウェーデン王国

面積　450,000km²（日本の約1.2倍）（世界57位）
人口　10,220,000人（世界91位）
公用語　スウェーデン語
首都　ストックホルム
民族　スウェーデン人　85%
　　　フィンランド人　5%
宗教　キリスト教プロテスタント・ルター派　80%
GDP　5,560億ドル（世界23位）
　　　1人当たりGDP　54,356ドル（世界12位）
通貨　スウェーデン・クローネ
政体　立憲君主制
識字率　99%

## Words and Phrases

次の１～5の語句の説明として最も近いものをａ～ｅから１つ選び、(　) 内に記入しなさい。

1. pinpoint ( )
2. rigorous ( )
3. pave the way ( )
4. human-caused ( )
5. fluctuation ( )

a. give precise information about
b. unstable change
c. resulting from the activity of people
d. provide a foundation
e. disciplined and detailed

## Summary

次の英文は記事の要約です。下の語群から最も適切な語を１つ選び、(　) 内に記入しなさい。

1-08

Scientists ( ) in America, Germany and Italy have shared the Nobel Physics Prize. Through their work on different aspects of ( ) change we now understand global warming better. Japan-born Syukuro Manabe developed a model to show ( ) between greenhouse gases and warming. This helped Klaus Hasselmann study changes in the ( ) and Giorgio Parisi explore fluctuations in the earth's ( ).

| atmosphere | based | climate | links | oceans |
|---|---|---|---|---|

2021年度のノーベル物理学賞は、「地球温暖化を予測する地球気候モデルの開発」で眞鍋淑郎プリンストン大学上席研究員とローマ・サピエンツア大学のジョルジョ・パリージ教授、マックス・プランク気象学研究所のクラウス・ハッセルマン教授に贈られた。

眞鍋氏は、1958年にアメリカ気象局の研究員として渡米した。1967年に高速コンピュータを使い、大気の運動との関係を定めるモデルを開発し、「$CO_2$が２倍に増えると地上気温が2.36度上昇する」との予測を明らかにした。さらに、1989年には、大気、海洋、陸上の気象が互いに与える影響を組み込んだ本格的な温暖化予測に成功した。

眞鍋氏は、地球を循環する大気や海の流れを物理法則に基づいて定式化し、数値で予測することを考えた。2002年から５期連続で世界最高の計算速度を達成した国産スーパーコンピュータ「地球シュミレーター」を駆使して、地球規模で降水量の分布や海流の状況などを詳しく把握できるようになった。眞鍋氏は、1931年生まれの90歳だが、「外に出て気候がどうなっているかを肌で感じること。何にでも好奇心を持つことが肝心だ」と力を込めて語っていた。

## Reading

1-09

# Nobel Prize in Physics Awarded for Study of Humanity's Role in Changing Climate

Three scientists received the Nobel Prize in Physics on Tuesday for work that is essential to understanding how the Earth's climate is changing, pinpointing the effect of human behavior on those changes and ultimately predicting the impact of global warming.

The winners were Syukuro Manabe of Princeton University, Klaus Hasselmann of the Max Planck Institute for Meteorology in Hamburg, Germany, and Giorgio Parisi of the Sapienza University of Rome.

1-10

"The discoveries being recognized this year demonstrate that our knowledge about the climate rests on a solid scientific foundation, based on a rigorous analysis of observations," said Thors Hans Hansson, chair of the Nobel Committee for Physics.

Complex physical systems, such as the climate, are often defined by their disorder. This year's winners helped bring understanding to what seemed like chaos by describing those systems and predicting their long-term behavior.

In 1967, Dr. Manabe developed a computer model that confirmed the critical connection between the primary greenhouse gas — carbon dioxide — and warming in the atmosphere.

1-11

That model paved the way for others of increasing sophistication. Dr. Manabe's later models, which explored connections between conditions in the ocean and atmosphere, were crucial to recognizing how increased melting of the Greenland ice sheet could affect ocean circulation in the North Atlantic, said Michael Mann, a climate scientist at Pennsylvania State University.

"He has contributed fundamentally to our understanding of human-caused climate change and dynamical mechanisms," Dr. Mann said.

About a decade after Dr. Manabe's foundational work,

Awarded：《大見出しの場合、受動態の be 動詞を省略する》
work：業績
pinpointing 〜：〜を特定する
predicting 〜：〜を予想する
Syukuro Manabe：眞鍋淑郎
Institute for Meteorology：気象学研究所
recognized：表彰される
rests on 〜：〜に基づく
observations：観測
disorder：無秩序
confirmed 〜：〜を確認した
atmosphere：大気
sophistication：洗練さ
ocean：大洋
crucial to 〜：〜にとって重要だ
ocean circulation：海洋循環
dynamical mechanisms：動的メカニズム

1-12

Dr. Hasselmann created a model that connected short-term climate phenomena — in other words, rain and other kinds of weather — to longer-term climate like ocean and atmospheric currents. Dr. Mann said that work laid the basis for attribution studies, a field of scientific inquiry that seeks to establish the influence of climate change on specific events like droughts, heat waves and intense rainstorms.

Dr. Parisi is credited with the discovery of the interplay of disorder and fluctuations in physical systems, including everything from a tiny collection of atoms to the atmosphere of an entire planet.

All three scientists have been working to understand the complex natural systems that have been driving climate change for decades, and their discoveries have provided the scaffolding on which predictions about climate are built.

1-13

The importance of their work has only gained urgency as the forecast models reveal an increasingly dire outlook if the rise in global temperature is not arrested.

Dr. Manabe is a senior meteorologist and climatologist at Princeton University. Born in 1931 in Shingu, Japan, he earned his Ph.D. in 1957 from the University of Tokyo before joining the U.S. Weather Bureau.

Dr. Hasselmann is a German physicist and oceanographer who greatly advanced public understanding of climate change through the creation of a model that links climate and chaotic weather systems. He is a professor at the Max Planck Institute for Meteorology in Hamburg.

Dr. Parisi is an Italian theoretical physicist who was born in 1948 in Rome and whose research has focused on quantum field theory and complex systems.

By Cade Metz, Marc Santora and Cora Engelbrecht
*The New York Times, October 7, 2021*

phenomena：現象
laid the basis for ～：～の基礎を築いた
inquiry：研究
is credited with ～：～で有名
interplay：相互作用
fluctuations：揺らぎ、変動
collection of ～：～の集まり
driving ～：～を推進してきた
scaffolding：足場
gained urgency：緊急性を増した
forecast：予想
outlook：見通し
arrested：阻止される
Shingu：和歌山県新宮市
Ph.D.：博士号
U.S. Weather Bureau：米国気象局
oceanographer：海洋学者
quantum field theory：「場の量子論」
complex systems：「複雑系」

## Exercises

### Multiple Choice

次の１～５の英文を完成させるために、ａ～ｄの中から最も適切なものを１つ選びなさい。

1. In 2021, three scientists received the Nobel Prize in Physics for their studies that laid the foundation of our knowledge of the Earth's
   - **a.** weather and how humanity studies it.
   - **b.** climate and how humanity influences it.
   - **c.** climate and how science affects it.
   - **d.** weather and how science develops it.

2. In 1967, Syukuro Manabe led the development of a computer model
   - **a.** proving the link between carbon dioxide and atmospheric warming.
   - **b.** providing for the Earth's formation.
   - **c.** confirming the connection between information and practice.
   - **d.** maintaining data on economic growth.

3. Syukuro Manabe examined links between ________________ conditions.
   - **a.** greenhouse gas and fossil fuel gas
   - **b.** global and local
   - **c.** oceanic and atmospheric
   - **d.** human and mechanical

4. Hasselmann's work differed from Manabe's by
   - **a.** denying climate change.
   - **b.** using scientific modelling.
   - **c.** analyzing ocean data.
   - **d.** linking short-term to long-term phenomena.

5. Giorgio Parisi linked planetary behavior to
   - **a.** disorder among scientists.
   - **b.** the stable nature of physics.
   - **c.** oceanography.
   - **d.** the interplay of atoms.

## True or False

本文の内容に合致するものにT（True）、合致しないものにF（False）をつけなさい。

(　　) **1.** Dr. Manabe is a senior weather forecaster.

(　　) **2.** Dr. Hasselmann is a German oceanographer.

(　　) **3.** Dr. Parisi is older than Dr. Manabe.

(　　) **4.** Dr. Manabe's work laid the foundation for the development of current climate models.

(　　) **5.** The winners' main work was done in Japan, Germany and Italy respectively.

## Vocabulary

次の英文は、Nobel Prize Organisation のホームページに掲載された *Nobel Prize in Physics*『ノーベル賞物理学』の記事の一部です。下の語群から最も適切な語を 1 つ選び、(　) 内に記入しなさい。

One complex system of vital importance to humankind is Earth's (　　　). Syukuro Manabe demonstrated how increased levels of (　　　) dioxide in the atmosphere lead to (　　　) temperatures at the surface of the Earth. In the 1960s, he led the development of physical models of the Earth's climate and was the first person to explore the interaction between radiation balance and the vertical transport of air masses. His work laid the foundation for the development of current climate models.

About ten years later, Klaus Hasselmann created a model that links (　　　) weather and climate, thus answering the question of why climate models can be reliable despite weather being (　　　) and chaotic. Around 1980, Giorgio Parisi discovered hidden patterns in disordered complex (　　　). His discoveries are among the most important contributions to the theory of complex systems.

"The discoveries being recognised this year demonstrate that our knowledge about the climate rests on a solid scientific foundation, based on a rigorous (　　　) of observations. This year's Laureates have all contributed to us gaining deeper insight into the (　　　) and evolution of complex physical systems," says Thors Hans Hansson, chair of the Nobel Committee for Physics.

| analysis | carbon | changeable | climate |
|---|---|---|---|
| increased | materials | properties | together |

Unit **3**

# ●五輪選手　米中間の対抗意識に巻き込まれる

2022年北京五輪スキー・ハーフパイプ女子で金メダルを獲得した「中国代表」のアイリーン・グー選手

The New York Times ／ Redux ／アフロ

## *Before you read*

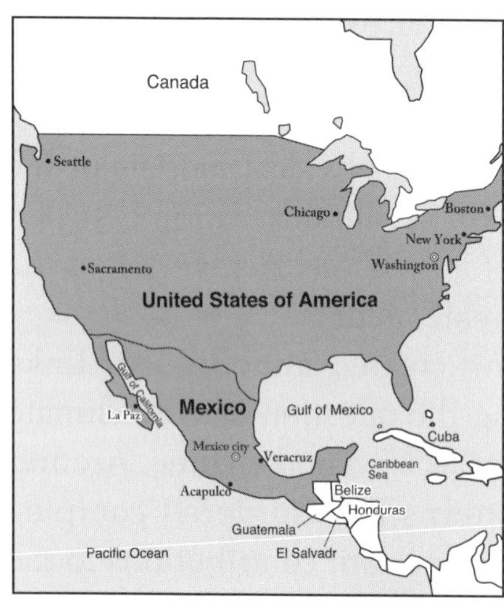


the United States of America
アメリカ合衆国

面積　9,628,000km²（日本の約25.5倍）（世界３位）
人口　332,000,000人（世界３位）
首都　ワシントン DC ／**最大都市**　ニューヨーク
公用語　なし、事実上は英語／**識字率**　93.5%
人種　白人　72.4%／ヒスパニック　18.5%
　　　黒人　12.7%／アジア系　4.8%
　　　ネイティブ・アメリカン　0.9%
宗教　キリスト教・カトリック　21%
　　　キリスト教・プロテスタント　58%
　　　ユダヤ教1.3%／イスラム教0.9%／無宗教　22.8%
GDP　18兆4,226億ドル（世界１位）
　　　１人当たり GDP　69,221ドル（世界９位）
通貨　US ドル／**政体**　大統領制・連邦制

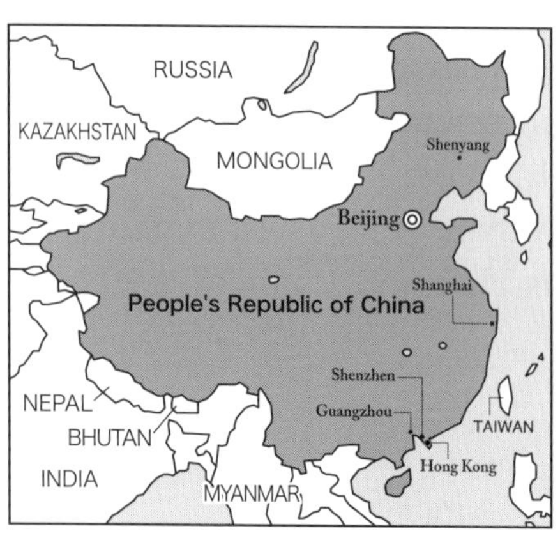


Beijing
北京市

People's Republic of China
中華人民共和国の首都
2008年８月８日に夏季オリンピックと2022年２月２日に冬季オリンピックが北京市で開催された。同一都市で、夏冬のオリンピックが開催されたのは、北京市が初めてだ。

面積　16,410.54km²
人口　21,705,000人（流動人口が3,649,000人）
　　　上海市に次ぐ中華人民共和国で第２位
公用語　中国語
民族　漢族が96%を占め、４%は55の少数民族で構成される
GDP　22968.6億元（１元＝19.32円）
　　　１人当たりの GDP　106,284元
通貨　元

## Words and Phrases

次の１～５の語句の説明として最も近いものをａ～ｅから１つ選び、(　　) 内に記入しなさい。

**1.** caught up (　　)
**2.** pundit (　　)
**3.** ungrateful (　　)
**4.** resurgent (　　)
**5.** surrender (　　)

**a.** failing to show appreciation
**b.** expert
**c.** give back
**d.** reviving or getting stronger
**e.** unintentionally involved

## Summary

次の英文は記事の要約です。下の語群から最も適切な語を１つ選び、(　　) 内に記入しなさい。

1-14 There was a lot of focus on Chinese American (　　　　) at the winter Olympics in Beijing. Some who competed for China received strong (　　　　) support when they won medals but (　　　　) negative comments in America. Some who were not so successful were (　　　　) online in China. All of them were made to think about their (　　　　) identities.

| attacked | competitors | faced | local | mixed |
|---|---|---|---|---|

国籍とは、その国に所属する個人の身分や資格のことをいい、「権利を得るための権利」と言われている。日本国籍によって、日本での参政権や出入国の自由などが憲法で保障される。日本では、1899年に施行された旧国籍法で、自らの意思で外国籍を取得した場合は日本国籍を失うと規定し、1950年施行の国籍法に受け継がれた。

世界の約75%の国が「重国籍」を容認している。国籍は、「国家への忠誠」と結びつけて捉えられていたが、現代では、個人の権利だと考え方が定着している。2019年のラグビー・ワールドカップの日本代表には15人もの外国出身の選手がいて、そのうち８人が日本国籍取得済みだった。ベナン出身の父を持つ八村塁選手、ハイチ出身の父の大坂なおみ選手は、日本人国籍を持つが、活動拠点は海外だ。

アメリカでは、重国籍が認められているが、中国では、日本同様、複数の国籍を持つことは難しいとされている。フリースタイルスキーのアイリーン・グー（谷愛凌）選手は、サンフランシスコで生まれ育ち、父が米国人、母は中国人だが、2019年15歳のときに米国籍から中国籍に変えた。米メディアからは「裏切り」との批判も出たが、中国の代表に転身し、中国に複数の金メダルをもたらし、金髪で北京語を話し、学歴重視の中国に、米国名門のスタンフォード大学の進学も決まり、母の祖国に貢献する道を選ぶという物語は、中国人の愛国心をかき立てたようだ。

## Reading

1-15

# The Olympians Caught Up in the U.S.-China Rivalry

> American athletes of Chinese descent at the Games are targets of patriotic and even nationalistic sentiment from both countries: sometimes adoring, sometimes hostile.

BEIJING — When the figure skater Nathan Chen won an Olympic gold medal for the United States, the state media in China, his parents' birthplace, practically ignored his victory.

When the Californian-born skater Beverly Zhu stumbled on the ice in her first appearance for China, Chinese social media users told her to "go back to America."

1-16

When Eileen Gu won gold skiing for China, people in China celebrated her as the nation's pride. But in the United States, where she was born and trained, some conservative political pundits called her ungrateful.

To be an American-born athlete of Chinese descent on sport's most prominent global stage is to be a lightning rod for patriotic, some say nationalistic, sentiment. Once held up as bridges linking the two countries, the Chinese American Olympians — and their successes and failures — are increasingly being seen as proxies in the superpowers' broader geopolitical tussle.

1-17

In China, a resurgent nationalism has meant that even among citizens, anyone airing even the mildest of criticisms can be accused of disloyalty. But the scrutiny of Chinese Americans is often harsh in other ways.

They are expected to show loyalty as part of a perceived extended Chinese family, yet are also distrusted as outsiders. Depending on the moment and mood, they can be shunned as traitors to the motherland or embraced as heroes who bring glory to the nation.

For the athletes, choosing which country to compete for is often a personal or practical decision. Having ties to

Caught Up in ～：～に巻き込まれる
Chinese descent：中国系
Games：五輪大会
patriotic：愛国心の強い
adoring：敬慕する
hostile：敵意がある
BEIJING：北京《記事の発信地》
state：国営の
Beverly Zhu：ビバリー・ズー 朱易
Eileen Gu：アイリーン・グー 谷愛凌
ungrateful：恥知らず
lightning rod：避雷針
proxies：代理人
geopolitical tussle：地政学的争い
disloyalty：不忠（な行為）、背信行為
scrutiny：精査
distrusted：不信感を抱かれる
traitors：裏切者
Having ties to ～：～と繋がりを持つこと《主語》

both the United States and China is also natural for Chinese Americans, many of whom grow up straddling two cultures, geographies and languages.

1-18

"When I'm in China, I'm Chinese and when I go to America, I'm American," Ms. Gu, 18, has often said in response to questions about her decision to compete for China. Ms. Gu, whose father is white and mother is Chinese, was born and raised in California by her mother. She speaks Chinese fluently and visited Beijing frequently as a child.

But worsening geopolitical tensions between Beijing and Washington have made maintaining the balancing act difficult for such athletes.

Many countries have for decades recruited foreign-born athletes to boost their chances of winning medals at the Olympics. Now China, too, is looking abroad for talent as well.

1-19

Around 30 athletes competing for China in this year's Games are naturalized Chinese citizens, with most playing for the men's and women's ice hockey teams.

Despite the outpouring of adulation in China, Ms. Gu is also walking a fine line. She has so far declined to answer repeated questions about whether she surrendered her United States passport.

Hu Xijin, a recently retired editor of Global Times, a brashly nationalist Chinese newspaper, warned Chinese propaganda organs on Sunday to moderate their praise of Ms. Gu, suggesting it was unclear which nation she would identify with as she got older.

By Amy Qin

*The New York Times ,February 17, 2022*

straddling 〜：〜にまたがって

in response to 〜：〜に答えて

chances：可能性

talent：才能ある人

naturalized：帰化した

outpouring：溢れかえること

adulation：賛辞

walking a fine line：順調に進む

surrendered 〜：〜を返還した、放棄した

Hu Xijin：胡錫進

Global Times：環球時報

brashly：厚かましいほど

identify with 〜：〜と一体感を持つ

# Exercises

## Multiple Choice

次の１～４の英文を完成させ、５の英文の質問に答えるために、ａ～ｄの中から最も適切なものを１つ選びなさい。

**1.** The writer suggested that Chinese state media

**a.** criticized Chen because he lost.
**b.** celebrated Chen's victory.
**c.** were interested in Chen's background.
**d.** ignored Chen as he was not born in China.

**2.** Beverly Zhu did not

**a.** compete for the country of her birth.
**b.** compete for China.
**c.** make any mistakes in her performance.
**d.** disappoint her Chinese fans.

**3.** The writer says Eileen Gu was

**a.** celebrated in America for her victory in skating.
**b.** criticized by some American conservatives.
**c.** grateful to China for the training she received there.
**d.** proud to have been born in China.

**4.** The Chinese media seem to support foreign-born athletes who

**a.** win and express Chinese patriotism.
**b.** try hard, even if they lose.
**c.** remain loyal to their country of birth.
**d.** offer individual and honest opinions.

**5.** Why are some people interested in Ms. Gu's passport?

**a.** They want to know if she competed for China or the US.
**b.** They want her to go back to America.
**c.** They want to know which country she is loyal to.
**d.** They want her to stop travelling until the Covid-19 crisis ends.

## True or False

本文の内容に合致するものにＴ（True）、合致しないものにＦ（False）をつけなさい。

(　　) **1.** Chinese American Olympians were generally expected to be loyal to China.

(　　) **2.** Despite worsening political relations between the United States and China, the two countries maintain high levels of trust.

(　　) **3.** China is unusual in recruiting foreign-born athletes.

(　　) **4.** Most of the naturalized Chinese competing at the Olympics were skiers.

(　　) **5.** Politics makes athletes' attempts to balance dual identities more difficult.

## Vocabulary

次の英文は、the New York Times に掲載された *Olympics Highlights: Medals Tally, Usually Predictable at Winter Games, Is More Open than Usual*『オリンピックのハイライト：メダルの数は、通常、冬季オリンピックでは予測可能だが、通常よりも公開されている』の記事の一部です。下の語群から最も適切なものを１つ選び、(　　) 内に記入しなさい。

Chloe Kim did it again, (　　　　) to another Olympic gold medal in the halfpipe. Just as she did four years ago, she opened the competition on Thursday by landing a score that (　　　　) could top. Kim knew it, too. When she got to the bottom of her first run, she put her hands to her head, fell on her knees in (　　　　) and laughed, as if she had shocked even herself. Her outburst at the bottom was a mix of joy and (　　　　). "I was like, I don't want to feel all this pressure of not being able to land my first safety run," she said. "So I just was overflowing with emotion when I was able to land it on the first go."

At the end of it all, Chen ended his routine at mid-ice, smiling and (　　　　), because he had done it. Finally, he had become the Olympic champion. His jet-fueled (　　　　) and a performance that raised goose bumps gave him the victory over three Japanese rivals who finished just behind him. With the victory, Chen, 22, shouted (　　　　) and clearly to all of the Beijing Games — and the world — that he has been the best skater around for more than three years and that nothing has changed. Four years ago, he finished fifth overall, (　　　　) his way back to that spot after finishing 17th in the short program.

| clawing | elated | joy | jumps |
|---|---|---|---|
| loudly | no one | relief | soaring |

Unit **4**

# ●民族主義と帝国主義に基づくプーチンのウクライナ戦争

# ●ロシア人　プーチン政権から逃れ、ウクライナ避難民と共にイスラエルに

2022年３月11日、クリミアのあるバス停前の広告。プーチン大統領は「ロシアは戦争を始めない、戦争を終わらす」と強調　ロイター／アフロ

## *Before you read*

Russian Federation
ロシア連邦

面積　17,098,246km²（日本の約45倍）（世界１位）
首都・最大都市　モスクワ
公用語　ロシア語／識字率　99.7%
人口　145,872,000人　（世界９位）
民族　スラブ人　82.7%／テュルク系　8.7%
　　　コーカサス系　3.7%／ウラル系　1.6%
宗教　ロシア正教会　63%／その他のキリスト教　4.5%
　　　イスラム教　6.6%／仏教　0.5%／ユダヤ教　0.6%
GDP　１兆6,572億米ドル（世界12位）
　　　１人当たりのGDP：11,289米ドル（世界65位）
通貨　ロシア・ルーブル
政体　共和制・連邦制

Ukraine　ウクライナ
ソビエト連邦より1991年8月24日独立

面積　603,700km²（日本の約1.6倍）（世界45位）
首都　キーウ
公用語　ウクライナ語／識字率　99.7%
人口　41,590,000人（南部クリミアを除く）
民族　ウクライナ人　77.8%／ロシア人　17.3%
　　　ベラルーシ人0.6%／モルドバ人、クリミア人、ユダヤ人等
宗教　ウクライナ正教会　76.5%
　　　その他のキリスト教　4.4%／ユダヤ教0.6%
GDP　5,450億300万米ドル
　　　１人当たりのGDP　13,128米ドル
通貨　フリヴニャ／政体　共和制

## Words and Phrases

次の１～５の語句の説明として最も近いものをａ～ｅから１つ選び、(　)内に記入しなさい。

| | | | |
|---|---|---|---|
| **1.** wage war | (　　) | **a.** so-called |
| **2.** assert | (　　) | **b.** make use of |
| **3.** assumption | (　　) | **c.** attack |
| **4.** alleged | (　　) | **d.** claim |
| **5.** take advantage of | (　　) | **e.** pre-existing or general idea |

## Summary

次の英文は記事の要約です。下の語群から最も適切な語を１つ選び、(　)内に記入しなさい。

1-20

While his (　　　　) believe nations should be based on individual rights and responsibilities, Putin emphasizes collectivist (　　　　). He justified his attack on Ukraine by (　　　　) it is part of Russia. Many Russians (　　　　) with him, and some feel they can no longer live in Russia. Fearing for their safety after making a movie (　　　　) Putin, two filmmakers fled to Israel.

claiming　　criticizing　　disagree　　nationalism　　opponents

ロシアのプーチン大統領は、2022年２月20日の北京冬季五輪閉幕の翌21日にウクライナ東部へのロシア軍派兵を命じ、24日に侵攻を開始した。ロシアは、2021年３月にウクライナとの国境地帯や、2014年に併合したウクライナ南部クリミアに大規模な軍部隊を集結させた。これは、ウクライナのゼレンスキー大統領のクリミア奪還に向けた国家戦略を採択したことに対するけん制の動きだった。10月下旬にはロシアはウクライナとの国境地帯に大規模な軍隊を再集結させ、増強を続けた。

12月中旬に、ロシアは、米国と北大西洋条約機構（NATO）を拡大せず、ロシアの「安全の保証」に関する条約案を提示し、ウクライナをNATOに加盟させないという要求を出した。この要求が拒否されれば「軍事技術的な対応」をとると警告した。バイデン大統領、マクロン大統領、ショルツ首相らも仲介に乗り出したが、不発に終わった。このウクライナ侵攻は、米国が主導するNATOが支えて来たヨーロッパの安全保障体制に、ロシアが武力で公然と挑戦したことになる。

ウクライナには、人口の約２割、800万人以上のロシア人が居住している。肥沃な農地に恵まれ、軍需・宇宙産業の拠点となっている。ロシアは帝政、ソ連時代にウクライナを支配し、両国は同じスラブ系民族で、ロシアを兄、ウクライナを弟とする「兄弟国家」と呼ばれて来た。しかし、長年に渡るロシアの圧迫は、ウクライナを欧米へと接近させている。米国、EU諸国、日本などが対ロシア経済制裁を発動しているため、ロシア経済は大打撃を受けているが、制裁を課した国々にも原油やガスのエネルギー価格の急騰で物価上昇が続いている。

## Reading

1-21

### Putin's War on Ukraine Is About Ethnicity and Empire

BRUSSELS — President Biden took office with the idea that this century's struggle would be between the world's democracies and autocracies.

But in waging war on Ukraine, President Vladimir V. Putin of Russia has been driven by a different concept, ethno-nationalism. It is an idea of nationhood and identity based on language, culture and blood — a collectivist ideology with deep roots in Russian history and thought.

Mr. Putin has repeatedly asserted that Ukraine is not a real state and that the Ukrainians are not a real people, but actually Russian, part of a Slavic heartland that also includes Belarus.

1-22

"Putin wants to consolidate the civilizational border of Russia, as he calls it, and he is doing that by invading a sovereign European country," said Ivan Vejvoda, a senior fellow at the Institute of Human Sciences in Vienna.

For Mr. Putin's opponents in Ukraine and the West, nations are built on civic responsibility, the rule of law and the rights of individuals and minorities, including free expression and a free vote.

"What Russia is doing is not just making war against an innocent nation here," said Timothy Snyder, a professor at Yale who has written extensively about Russia and Ukraine, but attacking assumptions about a peaceful Europe that respects borders, national sovereignty and multilateral institutions.

By Stephen Erlanger
*The New York Times, March 16, 2022*

Ethnicity：民族主義
took office：就任した
autocracies：専制主義、独裁政治
waging war：会戦
ethno-nationalism：民族国家主義
nationhood：国民性
collectivist：集産主義的《土地・生産手段などを国家が管理する》
asserted 〜：〜と主張した
consolidate 〜：〜を強化する
sovereign：独立国の
Institute of Human Sciences：人間科学研究所
Vienna：ウィーン
opponents：反対派
assumptions：仮定
multilateral institutions：多国間機関

1-23

### Russians flee Putin regime to join Ukraine refugees in Israel

AFP Rehovot, Israel — The moment Russian tanks rolled

regime：政権
refugees：避難民
AFP：AFP-JIJI《記事の配信会社：自社作成の記事ではなく配信会社から入手した記事》
rolled into 〜：〜に侵入した

into Ukraine, Russian filmmakers Anna Shishova-Bogolyubova and Dmitry Bogolyubov knew they had to leave Moscow.

"We were the next on the list," the couple said in their borrowed flat in Rehovot, a quiet Israeli city 20 kilometers (12 miles) south of Tel Aviv.

Once you're on the list of alleged "foreign agents," you face a life of "self-censorship or, sooner or later, prison," said Bogolyubov, who directed the German-financed 2019 documentary "Town of Glory".

1-24

The film portrays President Vladimir Putin's use of references related to the fight against Nazi Germany to establish his authority in Russian villages.

As its international isolation has deepened, Moscow has come to view all movies made with foreign financing with suspicion, including documentaries, and the couple said theirs was no exception.

"Over the past few years, we felt threatened. In the past few months in particular, people were spying on us and taking photographs on our film sets," Shishova-Bogolyubova said.

The couple decided to continue working in Russia but, taking advantage of their Jewish ancestry, they obtained Israeli citizenship just in case.

1-25

Since Russian troops invaded on February 24, nearly 24,000 Ukrainians have fled to Israel, some but not all taking advantage of the law, according to immigration ministry figures.

They have been joined by around 10,000 Russians, said an Israeli immigration official.

The wave of immigration from Ukraine and Russia over the past seven weeks is the largest Israel has seen since the early 1990s when the collapse of the Soviet Union prompted hundreds of thousands to seek a new life on the shores of the Mediterranean.

*The Japan Times, April 17, 2022*

- flat：アパート
- alleged ～：～と推定された（人物）
- self-censorship：自己検閲
- references：言及
- isolation：孤立
- with suspicion：疑って
- taking advantage of ～：～を利用する
- just in case：万が一に備えて
- immigration ministry figures：移民省の統計
- official：当局者
- collapse：崩壊
- prompted ～ to …：～に…するよう促した

## *Exercises*

### Multiple Choice

次の１～５の英文を完成させるために、ａ～ｄの中から最も適切なものを１つ選びなさい。

**1.** Putin's invasion of Russia reflects his belief that

**a.** his own race is more important than others.
**b.** Russia needs to recruit Ukrainian soldiers.
**c.** international borders must be respected.
**d.** nations are based on history rather than political choice.

**2.** Putin emphasizes

**a.** similarities among all the people of Europe.
**b.** similarities between the Ukrainians and Belarussians.
**c.** differences between the Russians and other Slavic people.
**d.** differences between freedom of expression and voting rights.

**3.** According to the article, Putin justified his attack on Ukraine by claiming

**a.** it is part of Russia.
**b.** it is next to Russia.
**c.** it is autocratic.
**d.** it is democratic.

**4.** Bogolyubov's documentary "Town of Glory" describes Putin's

**a.** imprisonment of foreign journalists.
**b.** patriotic war against Ukraine.
**c.** exploitation of nostalgia to increase his authority.
**d.** life as a solider during the Second World War.

**5.** Since the invasion of Ukraine, Israel has received thousands of refugees

**a.** who support the ongoing war.
**b.** from Ukraine but not Russia.
**c.** who are victims of the collapse of the Soviet Union.
**d.** from both Russia and Ukraine.

## True or False

本文の内容に合致するものにT（True）、合致しないものにF（False）をつけなさい。

(　　) **1.** With the collapse of the Soviet Union in 1990, many people migrated to Iraq.

(　　) **2.** Germany financially supported the film "Town of Glory."

(　　) **3.** The makers of "Town of Glory" applied for citizenship upon arrival in Israel.

(　　) **4.** Putin believes in ethno-nationalism based on language, culture and blood.

(　　) **5.** Putin wants to fortify the Russian border by invading Ukraine and Belarus.

## Vocabulary

次の英文は、読売新聞の The Japan News「えいご工房」に掲載された *Crisis escalates as migrants attempt to storm into Poland*『ポーランドへ流入試みる移民で危機深刻化』の記事の一部です。下の語群から最も適切な語を１つ選び、（　）内に記入しなさい。

WARSAW (AP) — Hundreds, if not thousands, of migrants sought to (　　　　) the border from Belarus into (　　　　) on Nov. 8, cutting razor wire fences and using branches to try and climb over them. The siege escalated a crisis along the European Union's eastern border that has been (　　　　) for months.

Poland's Defense Ministry posted a video showing an armed Polish officer using a (　　　　) spray through a fence at men who were trying to cut the (　　　　) wire.

A spokesman for Poland's security forces stressed that the "large groups of migrants ... are fully controlled by the Belarusian security services and army." He (　　　　) Belarusian President Alexander Lukashenko of acting to (　　　　) Poland and other EU countries to pressure the bloc into dropping its sanctions on Minsk. Those sanctions were put into place after Belarus (　　　　) down brutally on democracy protests.

| accused | chemical | cracked | destabilize |
|---|---|---|---|
| Poland | razor | simmering | storm |

Unit 5

# ●アブラモヴィッチの資産凍結でチェルシーが危機状態に

ロシアのウクライナ侵攻で、名門サッカー・クラブが危機に。チェルシーのホーム・スタジアム入口のロゴマーク　ロイター／アフロ

## *Before you read*

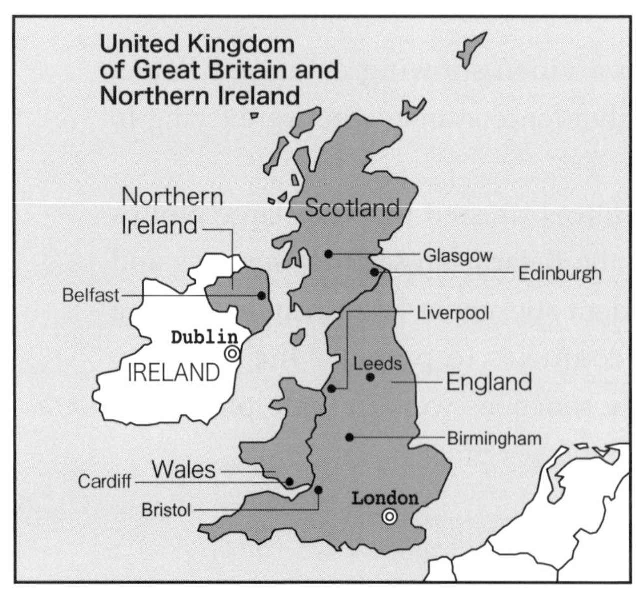


the United Kingdom of Great Britain and Northern Ireland
英国（グレートブリテン及びアイルランド連合王国）

面積　244,820km²（日本の本州と四国とほぼ同じ）（世界78位）
人口　67,530,000人（世界21位）
公用語　英語
首都　ロンドン
民族　イングランド人　5,500万人
スコットランド人　540万人
（北）アイルランド人　181万人
ウエールズ人　300万人
宗教　キリスト教　71.6%／イスラム教徒　2.7%
ヒンドゥ教　1.0%
GDP　2兆8,288億ドル（世界5位）／
1人当たりGDP　42,580ドル（世界22位）
通貨　UKポンド
政体　立憲君主制
識字率　99%

## Words and Phrases

次の１～５の語句の説明として最も近いものをａ～ｅから１つ選び、(　)内に記入しなさい。

1. text messages (　　)
2. holdings (　　)
3. untenable (　　)
4. austerity (　　)
5. dispense (　　)

a. short communications sent by smartphone
b. need to be very careful about money
c. distribute
d. impossible to maintain or defend
e. financial or property assets

## Summary

次の英文は記事の要約です。下の語群から最も適切な語を１つ選び、(　)内に記入しなさい。

1-26 Like many wealthy Russians (　　　　) to Putin, Roman Abramovich has had his assets frozen. This means he can sell (　　　　) Chelsea Football Club nor its players or (　　　　). The British government has promised that players and staff will still be (　　　　) and fans will still be able to watch matches. But this is a worrying and (　　　　) time for the club.

close　confusing　merchandise　neither　paid

ロマン・アブラモヴィッチは、1966年生まれのユダヤ系ロシア人の実業家である。３歳のときに両親を亡くし、孤児として育った。ソ連崩壊後の1992年26歳のとき、商売を始め、特に石油取引業で巨万の富を得た。34歳で、チュクチ自治管区の知事に選出され、８年間勤めた。ロシアの新興財閥オリガルヒの一人として、政治家や官僚との関係で存在を拡大させていった。知事就任３年後の2003年に、イングランドのサッカー・クラブのチェルシーを買収し、約160億円の負債を返済し、次々と有力選手を獲得し、アブラモヴィッチの名は、世界中に知られるようになった。

2022年２月24日にロシアのウクライナ侵攻が始まり、ウクライナ側の要請により、仲介者としてウクライナとロシアとの和平交渉に関与した。その際、アブラモヴィッチとウクライナ側の代表団の目の充血、顔や手の皮膚の剥がれる症状を訴え、毒物が投与されたとメディアは報道している。彼は、プーチン大統領やユダヤ人勢力との関係を保ちながら西側に根を下ろそうと努力し特異な立場をとって来た。

2022年３月12日にプレミア・リーグ側がアブラモヴィッチを失格処分にした。その後、英国政府は、チェルシー FC の運営継続を許可する特別ライセンスを発行し、アブラモヴィッチが取引から利益を得ない限り、クラブの売却を認める声明を出した。MLB カブスのオーナー、NFL ジェッツのオーナー、MLB ドジャースのオーナー・ベーリーとスイスの大富豪ヴィスらと組んだコンソーシアム等が買収に興味を示した。2022年５月にチェルシーがベーリーのコンソーシアムに42億5000万ポンド（約6,800億円）で売却され、政府の承認を得た。売却の純収益を慈善事業に寄付し、チェルシーへの貸付けの返済を求めないことを約束した。

## *Reading*

1-27

# Britain Freezes Assets of Roman Abramovich, Creating Crisis at Chelsea

Assets：資産

Chelsea：チェルシー《1905年設立のロンドン西部のフラムに本拠を置くプロサッカー・クラブ》

LONDON — For Chelsea F.C.'s players and coaches, the first snippets of information arrived in the text messages and news alerts that pinged their cellphones as they made their way to a private terminal at London's Gatwick Airport on Thursday morning.

alerts：通知《名詞》

pinged ～：～にピーンという音を出させた

made their way to ～：～に向かっていた

The British government had frozen the assets of their team's Russian owner, Roman Abramovich, as part of a wider set of sanctions announced against a group of Russian oligarchs. The action, part of the government's response to Russia's invasion of Ukraine, was designed to punish a handful of individuals whose businesses, wealth and connections are closely associated with the Kremlin. Abramovich, the British government said, has enjoyed a "close relationship" with Russia's president, Vladimir V. Putin, for decades.

sanctions against ～：～に対する制裁措置

oligarchs：オリガルヒ、新興財閥

1-28

The order applied to all of Abramovich's businesses, properties and holdings, but its most consequential — and most high-profile — effect hit Chelsea, the reigning European soccer champion, which was at that very moment beginning its journey to a Thursday night Premier League match at Norwich City.

properties：財産

holdings：持ち株

high-profile：注目を集める

Premier League：プレミア・リーグ

News reports and government statements slowly filled in some of the gaps: Abramovich's plans to sell the team were now untenable, and on hold; the club was forbidden from selling tickets or merchandise, lest any of the money feed back to its owner; and the team was prohibited — for the moment — from acquiring or selling players in soccer's multibillion-dollar trading market.

untenable：受け入れ難い

on hold：保留状態

lest ～：～しないように

for the moment：今のところ

1-29

And hour by nervous hour, one more thing became clear: Chelsea, one of Europe's leading teams and a contender for another Champions League title this season, was suddenly facing a worrisome future marked by austerity, uncertainty

contender：候補

austerity：緊縮財政

and decay.

Even as it announced its actions against Abramovich and six other Russian oligarchs, the government said it had taken steps to ensure Chelsea would be able to continue its operations and complete its season. To protect the club's interests, the government said, it had issued Chelsea a license allowing it to continue its soccer-related activities.

1-30

The license, which the government said would be under "constant review," will ensure that the team's players and staff will continue to be paid; that fans holding season tickets can continue to attend games; and that the integrity of the Premier League, which is considered an important cultural asset and one of Britain's most high-profile exports, will not be affected.

But the sanctions will put a stranglehold on Chelsea's spending and seriously undermine its ability to operate at the levels it has for the past two decades.

1-31

An uncertain future awaits, with the sanctions affecting everything from the money Chelsea spends on travel to how it dispenses the tens of millions of dollars it receives from television broadcasters.

At the club on Thursday morning, staff members were struggling to come to terms with what the government's actions would mean for them, their jobs and the team. Many club officials, including Chelsea's coach, Thomas Tuchel, a German, and Abramovich's chief lieutenant, the club director Marina Granovskaia, were still trying to understand what they could and could not do.

By Tariq Panja
*The New York Times, March 10, 2022*

decay：衰退
taken steps：措置を講じた
operations：活動
interests：利益
under "constant review"：「絶え間ない調査」の対象となる
integrity：完全性
put a stranglehold on ～：～を抑制する
undermine ～：～を損なう
dispenses ～：～を分配する
come to terms with ～：～を理解する
coach：監督
chief lieutenant：首席補佐官
director：代表

## Exercises

### Multiple Choice

次の１～５の英文を完成させるために、a～dの中から最も適切なものを１つ選びなさい。

**1.** The British government froze Roman Abramovich's assets due to

**a.** Chelsea's poor performances.
**b.** Russia's invasion of Ukraine.
**c.** his dealings on multi-million dollar trading markets.
**d.** corruption in Russian soccer.

**2.** The writer states that Chelsea owner Roman Abramovich

**a.** had been at school with Vladimir Putin.
**b.** was suspected of close connections with Russia's KGB.
**c.** was not the only Russian oligarch to be punished.
**d.** had actively supported the war against Ukraine.

**3.** Some Chelsea players and coaches were concerned about

**a.** their unpredictable future.
**b.** being accused of supporting Putin.
**c.** Abramovich's declining performance on the field.
**d.** the influence of Russian television on their club.

**4.** The British government issued Chelsea a license allowing it to continue

**a.** spending money as before.
**b.** competing in the Premier League.
**c.** playing soccer in empty stadiums.
**d.** paying staff, but not players.

**5.** Despite the sanctions, Britain's government considers Chelsea

**a.** a club dominated by Russians.
**b.** the best soccer team in Europe.
**c.** a burden on the economy.
**d.** of national cultural and economic significance.

## True or False

本文の内容に合致するものにT（True）、合致しないものにF（False）をつけなさい。

(　　) **1.** Roman Abramovich has had a good friendship with Vladimir Putin.

(　　) **2.** Roman Abramovich will sell Chelsea in the near future.

(　　) **3.** The British government froze the assets of seven Russian oligarchs.

(　　) **4.** Chelsea's players and coaches should still be able to complete their season.

(　　) **5.** Only the coach seems to know what the club is allowed to do.

## Vocabulary

次の1～8は、サッカーに関する英文です。下の語群の中から最も適当な語や語句を1つ選び、(　) 内に記入しなさい。

**1.** An attacking player attempts to kick the ball past the (　　　　) team's goalkeeper and between the goalposts to score a goal.

**2.** A (　　　　) saved a close-range shot from inside the penalty area.

**3.** A player takes a free kick, while the opposition form a (　　　　) in order to try to deflect the ball.

**4.** A goalkeeper (　　　　) to stop the ball from (　　　　) his goal.

**5.** A (　　　　) is when the same player makes three goals in one game.

**6.** Football is a game played between two teams of (　　　　) players using a round ball.

**7.** Players are cautioned with a (　　　　) card, and sent off with a (　　　　) card.

**8.** A player scores a penalty kick given after an offence is committed inside the (　　　　) area.

| | | | | |
|---|---|---|---|---|
| dives | eleven | entering | goalkeeper | hat trick |
| opposing | penalty | red | wall | yellow |

Unit 6

# ●大谷翔平選手　ア・リーグ MVP に誰もが納得

# ●大谷翔平選手　「神懸かりな」歴史的夜

大谷翔平選手が米国大リーグ野球のアメリカン・リーグ最優秀選手に満票で選ばれる　The New York Times ／ Redux ／アフロ

## *Before you read*

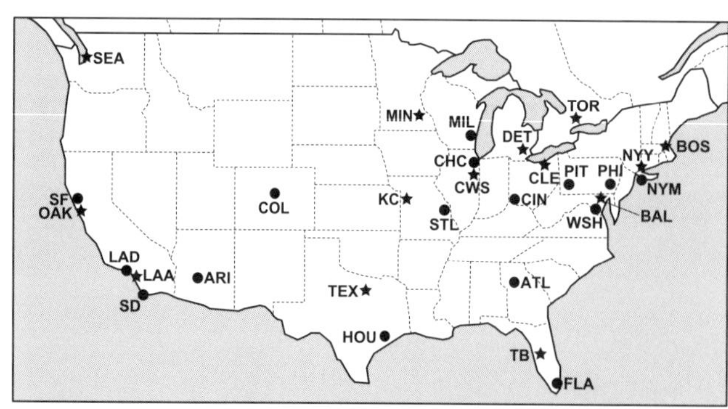


ナショナルリーグ ●

東地区
Atlanta Braves (ATL)
Florida Marlins (FLA)
New York Mets (NYM)
Philadelphia Phillies (PHI)
Washington Nationals (WSH)

中地区
Chicago Cubs (CHC)
Cincinnati Reds (CIN)
Houston Astros (HOU)
Milwaukee Brewers (MIL)
Pittsburgh Pirates (PIT)
St. Louis Cardinals (STL)

西地区
Arizona Diamondbacks (ARI)
Colorado Rockies (COL)
Los Angeles Dodgers (LAD)
San Diego Padres (SD)
San Francisco Giants (SF)

アメリカンリーグ ★

東地区
Baltimore Orioles (BAL)
Boston Red Sox (BOS)
New York Yankees (NYY)
Tampa Bay Rays (TB)
Toronto Blue Jays (TOR)

中地区
Chicago White Sox (CWS)
Cleveland Indians (CLE)
Detroit Tigers (DET)
Kansas City Royals (KC)
Minnesota Twins (MIN)

西地区
Los Angeles Angels of Anaheim (LAA)
Oakland Athletics (OAK)
Seattle Mariners (SEA)
Texas Rangers (TEX)

## Words and Phrases

次の１～５の語句の説明として最も近いものをａ～ｅから１つ選び、(　　) 内に記入しなさい。

1. slug (　　)
2. beat out (　　)
3. freed from (　　)
4. perch (　　)
5. possessed (　　)

a. position with a good view
b. no longer limited by
c. achieve a victory over
d. hit
e. completely and obsessively focused

## Summary

次の英文は記事の要約です。下の語群から最も適切な語を１つ選び、(　　) 内に記入しなさい。

1-32

Last season Shohei Ohtani was not (　　　　) one of the league's best hitters, but also his team's best pitcher. His Most Valuable Player (　　　　) from the American League (　　　　) his decision to remain a two-way player despite being advised (　　　　) it. And Ohtani has already made up for a (　　　　) start to this season by getting 12 strikeouts against the Astros.

against　　award　　justifies　　only　　slow

大谷翔平選手は、1994年７月５日に岩手県奥州市（旧水沢市）生まれの28歳だ。193cm の長身を生かして投手と打者を本格的に行う二刀流選手である。アマチュア時代、日本ハム時代、そしてエンジェルスに入団後も投打に大活躍している。投手としては、右投げで、最速165km/h を記録した。オーバースローから繰り出すストレート、フォークボール、スライダーを投げる。また、野手としても左打ちの外野手で、抜群の長打力はメジャーリーグ開幕後のエンジェルスの３試合連続本塁打を記録した。最長飛距離143m の長打力が称賛された。１塁まで3.8秒台の俊足で、強肩も兼ね備えている。

渡米４年目の2021年のアメリカン・リーグ最高殊勲選手 MVP に選ばれた。投打の「二刀流」で見せた歴史的な活躍に、投票権を持つ全米野球記者協会の30人の記者全員が１位票を投じる「満票」で選ばれた。渡米１年目には右肘、２年目の左膝の手術を経て、患部の不安が消えた４年目、打者で打率２割５分７厘、46本塁打、100打点、26盗塁、投手で９勝２敗、防御率3.18の成績を残した。さらに、リーグの区別なく活躍した選手を選ぶ「All MLB TEAM」の DH 部門で First Team に選ばれた。

2022年５月15日のアスレティック戦の５回に指名打者として出場し、大リーグ通算100号本塁打を放った。９月25日現在の打撃通算成績は、打率２割７分、打点92点、本塁打34本。投手としては26試合登板し、14勝、防御率2.47である。

## Reading

1-33

# Everyone Agrees: Shohei Ohtani Is the A.L.'s M.V.P.

Shohei Ohtani was extraordinary this season. Ohtani, the Los Angeles Angels' two-way star, smashed 46 home runs, drove in 100 runs and posted a .965 on-base plus slugging percentage, trailing only Toronto's Vladimir Guerrero Jr. in the American League. As if that wasn't impressive enough, Ohtani was also his team's best starting pitcher, amassing a 3.18 earned run average and 156 strikeouts in 130 1/3 innings over 23 starts.

1-34

On Thursday, Ohtani's historic efforts were rewarded with the A.L. Most Valuable Player Award. He joined the former Seattle Mariners star outfielder Ichiro Suzuki, the 2001 A.L. M.V.P., as the only Japanese players in Major League Baseball history to earn the award.

Ohtani received all 30 of the first-place votes for the award, which is presented annually by the Baseball Writers' Association of America. He beat out his fellow finalists, Guerrero, who received 29 second-place votes, and second baseman Marcus Semien, also of the Blue Jays, who received 24 third-place votes.

1-35

Throughout his career, even back in Japan, Ohtani has continually faced skepticism over his ability to remain a two-way player. It is hard enough being an everyday hitter in M.L.B., the top league with the best players in the world, let alone also serving as a starting pitcher.

But all along, even after having Tommy John surgery on his throwing elbow, his right, in 2018 and another elbow injury in 2020 forced him to miss nearly two seasons of pitching, he insisted on doing both. In his first season in M.L.B., in 2018 after signing with the Angels, Ohtani won the A.L. Rookie of the Year Award. Freed from the playing-time restrictions

A.L.：米大リーグのアメリカン・リーグ《他にナショナル・リーグがあり、両リーグの優勝チームがワールド・シリーズに出場》

M.V.P.：最高殊勲選手賞

two-way：投打の二刀流

100 runs：100打点

on-base plus slugging percentage：出塁率プラス長打率

Toronto：トロント・ブルージェイズ

starting pitcher：先発投手

amassing ～：～を記録する

earned run average：防御率

strikeouts：（奪）三振

outfielder：外野手

Baseball Writers' Association of America：全米野球記者協会

finalists：決勝戦出場者

Guerrero：ゲレーロ《48本のホームラン王》

Marcus Semien：マーカス・セミエン《ホームラン47本》

skepticism：懐疑的な見方

everyday hitter：常時出場の打者

let alone ～：～は勿論のこと

Tommy John surgery：側副靱帯再建術（肘の腱や靱帯の損傷・断裂に対する手術の様式）

imposed by his teams in the past, Ohtani was even better this year.

By James Wagner
*The New York Times, November 21, 2021*

1-36

## Shohei Ohtani 'was possessed' on historic night

HOUSTON — Shohei Ohtani was winless with a 5.92 ERA in six starts against the Houston Astros entering Wednesday's start.

Watching the superstar's performance from his perch in the dugout, Los Angeles Angels manager Joe Maddon could feel Ohtani was determined to change his fortunes against the Astros on Wednesday night.

He certainly did that.

The two-way star pitched perfect ball into the sixth inning, tied a career-best with 12 strikeouts and also had two hits and two RBIs to lead the Angels to a 6-0 shutout.

1-37

"He was possessed tonight," Maddon said. "That was a virtuoso performance from the beginning. He had a different look about him — and the stuff equaled the look."

Ohtani's big night gave him his first win of the season after entering the game 0-2 with a 7.56 ERA in his first two starts. He struck out six in a row at one point.

Maddon said it was the best he'd ever seen the 27-year-old pitch.

The reigning AL MVP made history Wednesday before he even took the mound. He batted twice in a six-run first inning as the Angels sent 10 to the plate — that made him the first starting pitcher since at least 1900 to bat twice in the first before throwing a pitch, according to the Elias Sports Bureau.

*The New York Post, April 22, 2022*

'was possessed'：「神懸かりな」

HOUSTON：ヒューストン《米国テキサス州最大の都市：NASA（米国航空宇宙局）の施設がある》

fortunes：運勢

career-best：自己最高

two RBIs：２打点

virtuoso performance：名人芸

big night：素晴らしい夜

struck out six：６三振を奪った

in a row：連続で

reigning：現在の、当代の

batted：打席に立った

six-run first inning：初回６得点

plate：ホーム・ベース《つまり打席》

Elias Sports Bureau：エリアス・スポーツ《北米主要リーグの記録を扱うデータ会社》

## *Exercises*

### Multiple Choice

次の１～５の英文を完成させるために、ａ～ｄの中から最も適切なものを１つ選びなさい。

**1.** Shohei Ohtani had an amazing season because he

- **a.** received his first career hit in MLB.
- **b.** earned his first win on the mound.
- **c.** was awarded Most Valuable Player.
- **d.** achieved all of the above.

**2.** Shohei Ohtani is known for

- **a.** being the first major league two-way player since Babe Ruth.
- **b.** his pitches of up to 90 kph.
- **c.** demonstrating wonderful poise.
- **d.** being nervous about pitching.

**3.** Shohei Ohtani received

- **a.** the N.L. M.V.P. in 2018.
- **b.** the N.L. Rookie of the Year Award in 2019.
- **c.** the A.L. M.V.P. in 2020.
- **d.** the A.L. M.V.P. in 2021.

**4.** Shohei Ohtani scored twelve strikeouts and two hits and two run batted ins

- **a.** to lose the Astros to 0 score.
- **b.** to lead the Athletics to a shutout.
- **c.** to lose the Athletics to 6 scores.
- **d.** to lead the Angels to 6 scores.

**5.** The abbreviation ERA stands for

- **a.** equal rights amendment.
- **b.** earned run average.
- **c.** emerging rookie award.
- **d.** excellent record achievement.

## True or False

本文の内容に合致するものにT（True）、合致しないものにF（False）をつけなさい。

(　　) **1.** Ichiro Suzuki, the former Seattle Mariners infielder, received the 2001 A.L. M.V.P.

(　　) **2.** Ohtani earned six more first-place votes than Marcus Semien.

(　　) **3.** Even in Japan, some people remain skeptical over his talent as a two-way player.

(　　) **4.** Ohtani had Tommy John surgery on his throwing elbow in 2020.

(　　) **5.** Ohtani's game against the Angels made it six stunning performances in a row.

## Vocabulary

次の英文は、The New York Times に掲載された *Japan's Perfect Game Drought Ends With a 19-Strikeout Masterpiece*『日本の完全試合も 19 奪三振で達成する』の記事の一部です。下の語群から最も適切なものを 1 つ選び、(　) 内に記入しなさい。

Roki Sasaki's (　　　) game was a long time coming, the first in the Japanese majors since 1994. But the wait turned out to be (　　　) it. Sasaki struck out 19 of the 27 men he faced, completing what would have to be described as one of the greatest games ever (　　　).

The 6-0 (　　　) for the Chiba Lotte Marines over the Orix Buffaloes on Sunday did not only break the Japanese record for (　　　) in a perfect game, but it also far (　　　) the major league mark of 14 by Matt Cain of the Giants in 2012 and Sandy Koufax for the Dodgers in 1965.

Sasaki, 20, struck out the third batter he faced in the first inning, then struck out the side in the second, third, fourth and fifth innings. The 13 (　　　) strikeouts is a Japanese baseball record.

It was the first complete game of Sasaki's young career, and even with the high strikeout total it required only 105 pitches. "The big thing today was getting ahead in counts, being able to throw strikes," Sasaki told Kyodo News. "Now I want to do my (　　　) to pitch well next time."

| best | consecutive | perfect | pitched |
|---|---|---|---|
| strikeouts | surpassed | victory | worth |

Unit 7

# ●日本の労働組合は男性中心、女性指導者の誕生で変わるのか

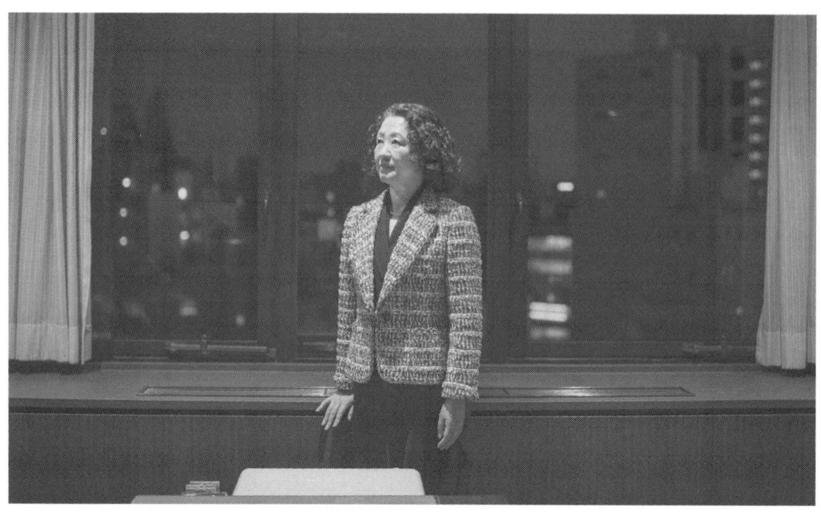

男性中心社会の日本の労働組合の中で最大規模の日本労働組合総連合会（連合）初の女性トップになった芳野友子さん。果たして「組合」はどう変わるのか？

The New York Times ／ Redux ／アフロ

## *Before you read*

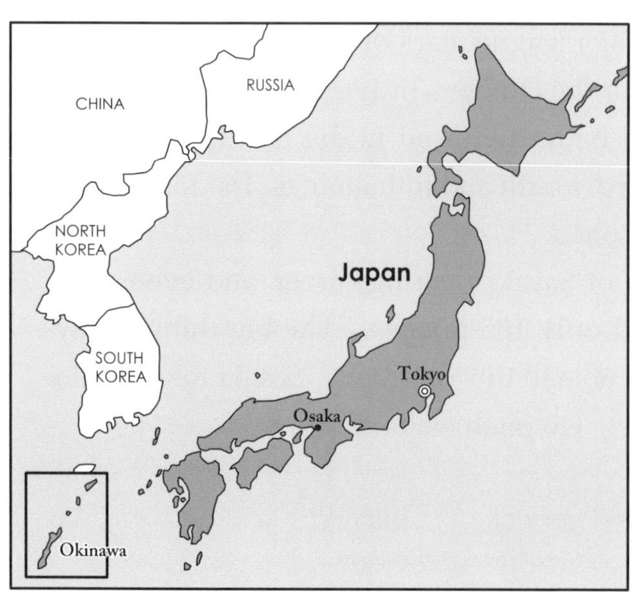


Japan
日本国

面積　377,961.73km²（世界61位）
人口　126,860,000人（世界11位）
　　日本民族　98.5%
　　朝鮮人　0.5%
　　中国人　0.4%
首都　東京都
最大都市　大阪市（昼間人口）
　　　　横浜市（夜間人口）
　　　　東京都23区部
GDP　４兆9,718億ドル（世界３位）
　　１人当たりのGDP　39,304ドル（世界26位）
通貨　円
公用語　なし、事実上日本語
宗教　無宗教信者　52%
　　仏教　35%／神道　４%
　　キリスト教　2.3%
政体　立憲君主制
識字率　99.8%

## Words and Phrases

次の1～5の語句の説明として最も近いものをa～eから1つ選び、(　)内に記入しなさい。

1. failing (　　)
2. be tempered with (　　)
3. stand up for (　　)
4. dwindle (　　)
5. reluctant (　　)

a. give support to
b. get smaller or weaker
c. unwilling
d. weakness
e. be softened or weakened by

## Summary

次の英文は記事の要約です。下の語群から最も適切な語を1つ選び、(　)内に記入しなさい。

1-38 Dominated by men, Japan's unions have (　　　). Rather than increase membership, (　　　) about job security led to a fall in numbers. There are now more (　　　) employees, many of them female. Feeling that their interests have been (　　　), most don't join unions. The first female leader of Japan's largest union hopes that (　　　) on women's issues will bring about a revival.

declined　fears　focusing　ignored　non-regular

2021年10月に芳野友子氏が、日本最大の労働組合である日本労働組合総連合会（連合）の8代目会長に就任した。組合員は、6,991,000人いる。女性では初と言われているが、彼女の就任1年前の2020年7月30日に全労連の議長に小畑雅子氏が就任していて、小畑氏が女性初になる。芳野友子氏が18歳のとき、ミシンの会社JUKIに入社し、16年後にJUKI労働組合委員長、その5年後に日本労働組合総連合会副会長に就任した。芳野氏は、企業や職場の労働組合が男性中心の世界であることに気づき、組合内に女性委員会を発足させ、男女均等待遇に向けた取り組みを行ってきた。2021年10月に連合会長の神津里季生氏の任期満了に伴い、「女性」「中小企業出身」「高卒たたき上げ」に合致する芳野氏が就任した。

2021年3月に開催された世界経済フォーラムで、各国における男女格差を測るジェンダー・ギャップ指数が発表された。この指数は、「経済」「政治」「教育」「健康」の4つの分野のデータから作成され、0が完全不平等、1が完全平等を示している。日本は、経済分野で0.604、政治は0.061、教育0.983、健康0.973で政治分野が極端に低く、国会議員の女性割合は、9.9%に過ぎない。総合スコアは、0.656で、順位は、156か国中120位で、先進国の中では最低レベルだ。1位アイスランドの0.892、2位フィンランド0.861、3位ノルウエー0.849で、アジアではタイの79位、インドネシア87位、韓国102位、中国107位だ。

## Reading

1-39

# Japan's Unions 'Are Built Around Men.' Can a Female Leader Change That?

TOKYO — Women have never found a welcoming home in Japan's labor unions. Sexism is entrenched. Problems like wage discrimination and sexual harassment at work are often ignored.

So when Japan's largest association of labor unions, known as Rengo, appointed its first female leader last October, the excitement was tempered with a heavy dose of skepticism.

The new chief, Tomoko Yoshino, knows the feeling well: After decades in the labor movement, she understands the failings of Japanese unions as well as anyone. But she's confident that she can make her appointment a powerful tool for reform.

1-40

To recruit female workers, unions will need to fight for measures that help women manage both their jobs and the heavy expectations they face outside work, including standing up for women facing sexual harassment and discrimination and pushing companies to provide more help with child care.

Japan has one of the world's worst records on gender equality, placing 120th out of 156 countries in a ranking by the World Economic Forum, even after years of government promises to help women "shine."

1-41

The problems with Japanese unions don't end with their treatment of women. While interest in labor groups has surged in the United States in recent years, they have become increasingly marginalized and irrelevant to many Japanese workers, said Kazunari Honda, a professor of human resources management at Mukogawa Women's University who studies gender in the labor movement.

It wasn't always that way. From the end of World War II through the 1970s, unions represented over 30 percent of Japanese workers.

Unions：労働組合
Sexism：性差別
entrenched：定着した
wage discrimination：賃金差別
ignored：無視される
Rengo：「連合」《日本労働組合総連合会の略称》
tempered with ～：～で和らげられた、軽減された
Tomoko Yoshino：芳野友子《出身母体は「ものづくり産業労働組合」》
as anyone：他の誰よりも
pushing ～ to …：～に…するよう促す
child care：育児
World Economic Forum：世界経済フォーラム《1971年設立の国際機関で毎年ダボス会議を開催》
don't end with ～：～だけに止まらない
marginalized：軽視される
irrelevant to ～：～とは無関係な
human resources management：人事管理(学)

But that number began to dwindle as the '70s energy crisis forced companies to downsize. When economic growth ground to a halt in the 1990s, membership plunged further. Workers, fearing layoffs, became more conservative in their demands, trading gains in pay and working conditions for job stability. Strikes, once a common tactic, largely disappeared.

1-42

Today, unions represent just 17 percent of Japan's work force, making it difficult for them to effect meaningful change.

As unions' influence has waned, another force in Japan's economy has been on the rise: non-regular workers, who fall outside the country's traditional model of jobs for life.

Since the 1980s, the number of non-regular workers in Japan has more than doubled, to almost 37 percent from 16 percent — some 20.6 million workers — in 2021. Nearly half are women, who have become disproportionately represented among non-regular employees as the percentage of female workers under 65 rose nearly 20 percent over the last several decades.

1-43

Unions have long been reluctant to include non-regular workers because the organizations are focused on protecting the prerogatives of their "regular" counterparts: better benefits and higher salaries.

For temporary workers, many of whom frequently switch employers, there is little incentive to commit to a group organized around a workplace they may soon leave.

Encouraging those workers to organize, Ms. Yoshino said, will require Rengo — which is known as the Japanese Trade Union Confederation in English and has about seven million members — to invest more in strengthening unions based around industries, not enterprises.

By Ben Dooley and Hisako Ueno
*The New York Times, February 16, 2022*

ground to a halt：止まった
layoffs：一時解雇
trading ～ for …：～と…とを交換する
gains in pay and working conditions：賃金と労働条件
job stability：雇用の安定
tactic：戦術
fall outside ～：～から外れる
for life：終身の
disproportionately：つり合いが取れないほど
reluctant to ～：～するのに消極的
prerogatives：特権
counterparts：《この場合は労働者》
temporary：一時（的）・短期の
incentive：動機付け
require Rengo：《require Rengo to 不定詞と続く》
invest in ～：～に投資する

## Exercises

### Multiple Choice

次の１～５の英文を完成させるために、ａ～ｄの中から最も適切なものを１つ選びなさい。

**1.** Tomoko Yoshino is

- **a.** reluctant to make too many changes.
- **b.** Rengo's English spokesperson.
- **c.** a former professor of gender studies.
- **d.** an experienced member of the labor movement.

**2.** According to the article, Japan is notorious for

- **a.** racial discrimination.
- **b.** gender inequality.
- **c.** economic harassment.
- **d.** job instability.

**3.** Japan's labor unions declined in the 1990s because of

- **a.** global inflation.
- **b.** economic stagnation.
- **c.** domestic deflation.
- **d.** energy-related problems.

**4.** As they want to protect their privileges, Japan's labor unions have been unwilling to

- **a.** admit full-time employees.
- **b.** draw in part-timers.
- **c.** demand higher salaries.
- **d.** press for better benefits.

**5.** Tomoko Yoshino plans to

- **a.** double union membership.
- **b.** recruit another 27 million members.
- **c.** change to an industry-based model.
- **d.** invest more money in female-dominated enterprises.

## True or False

本文の内容に合致するものにT (True)、合致しないものにF (False) をつけなさい。

( ) **1.** Rengo is translated as the Japanese Labor Union Confederation in English.

( ) **2.** By 2021, Japan's non-regular workers had decreased to around 20 million.

( ) **3.** Japan's unions face problems such as sexual harassment and wage discrimination.

( ) **4.** According to Professor Honda, unions have grown in importance in Japanese society.

( ) **5.** It is suggested that Yoshino will focus more on female and part-time workers.

## Vocabulary

次の英文は、読売新聞の The Japan News「えいご工房」に掲載された *Biden nominates Jackson to top court*『バイデン米大統領、ジャクソンを連邦最高判事に指名』の記事の一部です。下の語群から最も適切なものを１つ選び、( ) 内に記入しなさい。

U. S. President Joe Biden on Feb. 25 nominated federal appeals court Judge Ketanji Brown Jackson to the Supreme ( ), the first ( ) woman selected to serve on a court that once declared her race ( ) of citizenship and endorsed American ( ).

Introducing Jackson at the White House, Biden declared, "I believe it's time that we have a court that reflects the full talents and ( ) of our nation."

With his ( ) standing alongside, the president praised her as having "a ( ) understanding that the law must work for the American people."

In Jackson, Biden delivered on a campaign promise to make the ( ) appointment and further diversify a court that was made up entirely of white men for almost two centuries.

| black | court | historic | greatness |
|---|---|---|---|
| nominee | pragmatic | segregation | unworthy |

Unit **8**

# ●シンガポール 「不当感」の増大で死刑反対意見強まる

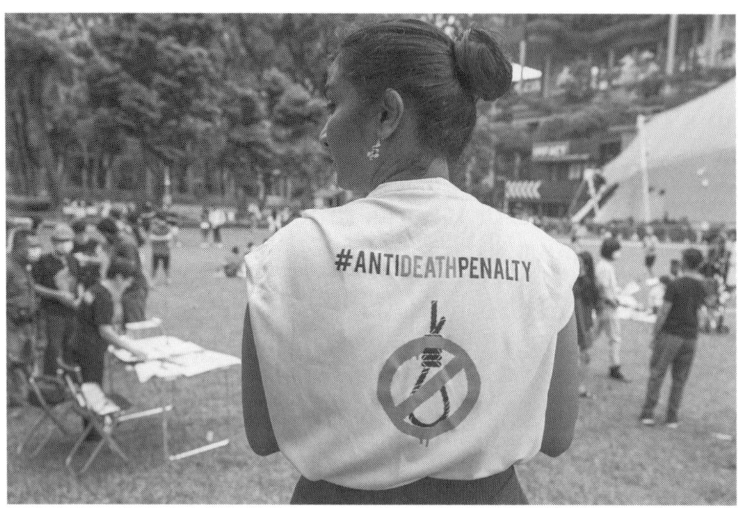


シンガポールの「スピーカーズ・コーナー」で「死刑反対」を訴えるＴシャツを着た女性 AFP／WAA

## *Before you read*

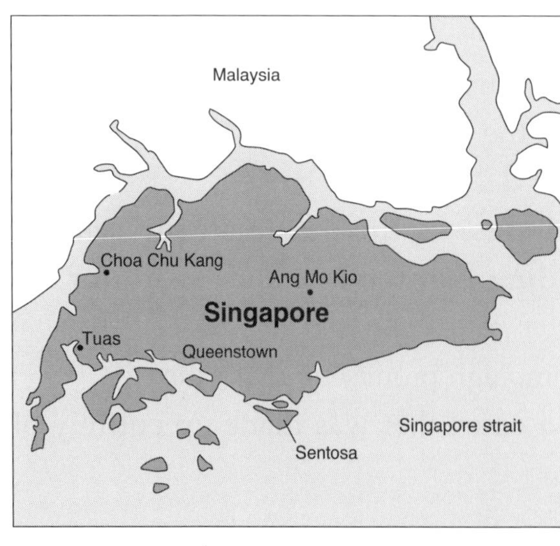


Republic of Singapore
シンガポール共和国
1965年８月９日マレーシアより独立

面積　720km²（東京23区とほぼ同じ）
人口　5,850,000人
民族　中国系　74%／マレー系　14%
　　　インド系　7.9%／その他　1.4%
公用語　国語はマレー語　12.2%
　　　中国語　50%／英語　32.3%
　　　タミル語　3.3%
GDP　3,399億8,100万ドル（世界38位）
　　　１人当たりのGDP　59,795ドル
通貨　シンガポール・ドル
宗教　無宗教信者　17%
　　　仏教　33%／イスラム教　15%
　　　キリスト教　18%／ヒンドゥ教　５%
政体　立憲共和制
識字率　97%

## Words and Phrases

次の１～５の語句の説明として最も近いものをａ～ｅから１つ選び、(　　) 内に記入しなさい。

| | | |
|---|---|---|
| **1.** clemency | (　　) | **a.** argue against |
| **2.** on death row | (　　) | **b.** become friends with |
| **3.** fall in with | (　　) | **c.** waiting to be executed |
| **4.** marginalized | (　　) | **d.** outlying and disadvantaged |
| **5.** critique | (　　) | **e.** mercy |

## Summary

次の英文は記事の要約です。下の語群から最も適切な語を１つ選び、(　　) 内に記入しなさい。

1-44

Singapore continues to (　　　　) drug-traffickers. The government argues that its (　　　　) policy keeps people safe. But (　　　　) about the fairness of the death penalty are growing. On death row for carrying a small quantity of drugs, Nagaenthran Dharmalingam claimed to have been (　　　　) into crime. His supporters point out that his IQ is very low. But his final appeal was (　　　　).

doubts　　execute　　forced　　rejected　　severe

シンガポールの領土は、埋立てにより拡大されてきた。事実上１つの都市から構成される都市国家である。教育、娯楽、金融、ヘルスケア、人的資本、イノベーション、物流、製造・技術、観光、貿易・輸送は世界的な中心にある。世界で最も「テクノロジー対応」国家（WEF)、国際会議のトップ都市（UIA)、「投資の可能性が最も高い」都市（BERI)、最も安全な国、最も競争力のある経済などが国際ランキングで上位に格付けされている。さらに、シンガポールは、購買力平価による１人当たり国内総生産（GDP）が世界で２番目に高く、国連人間開発指数で９位である。2020年のシンガポールの一人当たりの実質国民総所得 GNI は86,480ドルである。

シンガポール島嶼には２世紀に定住が始まり、1400年頃マラッカ王国が建国された。1942年から1945年まで日本軍に占領されたが、1959年にイギリスより自治権を獲得し、自治州になる。1963年にマレーシアが独立し、1965年マレーシアより分離し、シンガポール共和国として独立した。多文化主義及び文化多様性があり、560万人の人口の38%は、永住者及びその他外国籍の人である。シンガポール人は中国系74.1%、マレー系13.4%、インド系9.2%、大部分は２言語使用者であり、第２母語として英語を使用する。

シンガポールの法体系はイングランド法を基礎としている。刑事法や取締法規については一般的に厳格であり、身体刑と死刑が実施されている。世界的にも厳しい死刑制度を維持している。薬物に関する犯罪については厳格で、麻薬の密輸で有罪になった時は死刑のみが適用されたため、入国カードにも「麻薬密輸者は死刑」と警告文が書いてある。外国人の麻薬密売業者が死刑になった事例が存在し、死刑廃止国との間で外交問題に発展したことがある。

## Reading

1-45

# Singapore hardens opinion against death penalty as 'sense of injustice' grows

against ～：～反対の
'sense of injustice'：「不当感」

The news was delivered in just a few cold sentences. An appeal for clemency for Nagaenthran Dharmalingam, a man on death row whose case has prompted a global outcry, had failed.

"Please be informed that the position...remains unchanged" wrote Singapore president's principal private secretary, in a letter to Nagaenthran's family: "The sentence of death therefore stands."

clemency：恩赦
man on death row：死刑囚
outcry：抗議
sentence of death：死刑判決
stands：有効だ

1-46

Nagaenthran's relatives and supporters have campaigned tirelessly for his life to be spared. He was arrested in 2009, aged 21, for attempting to smuggle a small amount of heroin — about three tablespoons — into Singapore and has since spent more than a decade on death row. His lawyer has argued that he has an IQ of 69, a level recognised as indicating a learning disability, and should be protected from execution under international law. Nagaenthran has said he was coerced into carrying the drugs.

Nagaenthran's case has appalled rights groups, and provoked an outcry from voices around the world — from billionaire businessman Richard Branson, a critic of the death penalty, to EU representatives and UN experts. Domestically, it has also prompted some younger Singaporeans to question a system that the government has long claimed makes the city state "one of the safest places in the world".

smuggle ～ into …：～を…に密輸する
IQ：知能指数
learning disability：学習障害
execution：死刑執行
coerced into ～：～するよう強要される
rights groups：人権団体
city state：都市国家《シンガポールのこと》

1-47

Death penalty cases are rarely reported in any detail in Singapore's tightly controlled media, but Nagaenthran's story has been shared widely online. Isaac Chiew, a 22-year-old university student, said he hadn't thought very much about the death penalty, until he came across Nagaenthran's case on Instagram. "Reading all the details really made me feel this sense of injustice," he says. He began to read about others

Instagram：インスタグラム《写真やビデオを共有するソーシャル・ネットワーキング・サービス》

on death row, and was struck by stories of people who were condemned to death simply for falling in with the wrong crowd or making a mistake.

1-48

Profiles of some death row inmates shared online by campaigners show they are not big time criminals, but rather men from marginalised communities who have faced poverty, or struggled with addiction.

"Social media has allowed us to centre the voices of death row prisoners and their families," says Jolovan Wham, a human rights activist.

In a rare protest this month, more than 400 people turned out at Speakers' Corner at Hong Lim park, the only place where demonstrations are permitted in Singapore, to call for executions to be halted.

1-49

Kirsten Han, a journalist and activist who has spent a decade campaigning against the death penalty, believes its likely the highest turn out ever seen at such a demonstration. The message, too, was different.

"Previously a lot of other death penalty events might have been focused on - give this person a chance," said Han. But protesters were now critiquing the whole system. They weren't, she added, just expressing pity for any one person; they were calling for abolition of the death penalty. Most of the attendees were young Singaporeans.

The government argues that capital punishment is the most effective deterrent against crime — an idea debunked by criminological research, she adds.

By Rebecca Ratcliffe

*The Guardian News & Media Ltd, April 13, 2022*

condemned to death：死刑宣告される
falling in with ～：～に加わる
inmates：入獄者
big time：一流の、大物の
marginalised：疎外された
addiction：依存症
human rights activist：人権活動家
turned out：集まった
Speakers' Corner：スピーカーズ・コーナー《野外での演説、討論や議論が可能なエリア》
different：今までとは異なる
this：ある特定の、これこれの
They weren't：以前はそうではなかった
abolition：廃止
capital punishment：死刑
deterrent：抑止力
debunked by ～：～によって虚偽だと暴かれる
criminological：犯罪学の

# Exercises

## Multiple Choice

次の、１～４の英文を完成させ、５の英文の質問に答えるために、ａ～ｄの中から最も適切なものを１つ選びなさい。

**1.** Capital punishment is ________________ in Singapore.

- **a.** no longer used
- **b.** carried out
- **c.** to be reintroduced
- **d.** hardly used

**2.** Nagaenthran Dharmalingam's case has been globally discussed because of his

- **a.** frequent trafficking in narcotics.
- **b.** long-term addiction to drugs.
- **c.** violent criminal methods.
- **d.** weak mental capacity.

**3.** Nagaenthran's lawyer claims that ________________ violates international law.

- **a.** giving the death penalty to drug-traffickers
- **b.** executing people with learning disabilities
- **c.** keeping prisoners on death row for a decade
- **d.** allowing someone to carry drugs

**4.** Many death row prisoners come from

- **a.** powerful communities.
- **b.** influential communities.
- **c.** rich communities.
- **d.** powerless communities.

**5.** Who is described as campaigning against capital punishment for ten years?

- **a.** Richard Branson.
- **b.** Jolovan Wham.
- **c.** Isaac Chiew.
- **d.** Kirsten Han.

## True or False

本文の内容に合致するものにT（True）、合致しないものにF（False）をつけなさい。

( ) **1.** In a letter to Nagaenthran's family, the president's principle private secretary said the death penalty is not in force anymore.

( ) **2.** Nagaenthran was arrested for taking heroin about three years ago.

( ) **3.** Nagaenthran's story has spread online in Singapore.

( ) **4.** Hong Lim Park's Speakers' Corner is one of several places for demonstrations in Singapore.

( ) **5.** The Singaporean government argues that the death penalty is the most effective measure against crime.

## Vocabulary

次の１～８は、「法律」に関する英文です。日本文に合わせて、適当な語を下の語群から１つ選び、（ ）内に記入しなさい。

**1.** 彼は、詐欺容疑で逮捕された。
He was ( ) on suspicion of fraud.

**2.** 彼は、有罪と判決が下されたが、すぐに上告した。
He was found ( ) but appealed immediately.

**3.** 彼は、心神喪失の理由で無罪と判決が下された。
He was ( ) by reason of insanity.

**4.** 多くの国は、死刑を廃止した。
Many countries have abolished ( ).

**5.** 地方裁判所は、彼に無期懲役を言い渡した。
The district court sentenced him to ( ).

**6.** 裁判所は、彼に懲役２年、執行猶予３年の判決を下した。
The court gave him two years' imprisonment with a three years' ( ).

**7.** 死刑が、終身刑に減刑された。
The sentence of death was ( ) into life imprisonment.

**8.** 彼は、刑務所で６年間務めた後で仮釈放された。
He was ( ) after serving 6 years in prison.

| | | | |
|---|---|---|---|
| acquitted | arrested | capital punishment | commuted |
| guilty | life in prison | paroled | stay of execution |

Unit **9**

# ●不平等が野放しの富裕国の国民は不幸になる
# ●超金持ちでも相続時に悲惨な目に

2022年６月21日、過去30年で最大規模の鉄道ストライキが英国で実施され、乗客はただ待つのみ
ロイター／アフロ

## *Before you read*

### Questions

**1.** What do you think the article will be about?

この記事は何の話題についてだと思いますか？

**2.** Do you think rich people are generally happier than poor people?

全般的に、裕福な人は貧しい人より幸せだと思いますか？

## Words and Phrases

次の１～５の語句の説明として最も近いものをａ～ｅから１つ選び、(　　) 内に記入しなさい。

**1.** run rampant (　　)
**2.** puncture (　　)
**3.** feed into (　　)
**4.** manipulate (　　)
**5.** void (　　)

**a.** support or concur with
**b.** damage or put a hole in something
**c.** deceive or exploit
**d.** gap or empty space
**e.** get out of control

## Summary

次の英文は記事の要約です。下の語群から最も適切な語を１つ選び、(　　) 内に記入しなさい。

1-50

According to (　　　　) from Britain and India, when inequality increases, national (　　　　) decreases. It is (　　　　) enough that large wealth gaps tend to make poorer people unhappy. What is interesting, however, is that they (　　　　) to make rich people happier. One therapist has found that her wealthy clients often feel suspicious, (　　　　) and bored.

aimless　　data　　fail　　obvious　　satisfaction

収入や資産が増えれば、幸せになれるのか？という幸福度と収入の関係について調べたデータがある。幸福度と収入は比例するが、年収75,000米ドル（約800万円）で幸福度はほぼ頭打ちになるということが、ノーベル経済学賞受賞者のダニエル・カーネマン教授らによって発表されている。日本でも内閣府が年収と幸福度に関する調査結果を発表している。2019年の「満足度・生活の質に関する調査」では、１万人を対象に世帯年収別に主観的な満足度の変化を比べている。この調査によると、年収500万円以上700万円未満の人の幸福度は平均5.91、年収700万円以上1,000万円未満の人の幸福度は6.24で、0.33の差が開いているが、年収1,000万円以上2,000万円未満の幸福度は6.52で年収700万円以上1,000万円未満との差は0.28となっている。日本では、年収3,000万円が幸福度のピークのようだ。

それでは、なぜ収入が上がると幸福度が頭打ちになるのかという疑問が出た。お金によって満たされるのは、あくまでも「満足度」だけで、「幸福度」ではないということだ。社会科学者マイケル・ノートン氏の調査によると、「モノ」にお金を使うより「体験」に使う方が、幸福度が高いという結論が出ている。国連が毎年「世界幸福度ランキング」という調査結果を発表している。GDP、平均余命、社会的寛容さ、社会的支援、自由度、腐敗度といった要素をもとに幸福度を分析している。2020年の日本の幸福度は、156か国中62位である。GDP３位の経済大国である日本の順位が低いことは、経済指標だけでは豊かさや幸福度は表せないことを表している。幸福度の順位は、１位フィンランド、２位デンマーク、３位スイス、とヨーロッパの国々で占めている。

## Reading

1-51

# Rich countries that let inequality run rampant make citizens unhappy, study finds

inequality：不平等、格差
run rampant：野放しになる

Countries that allow economic inequality to increase as they grow richer make their citizens less happy, a new study shows.

Until now, researchers have believed that inequality was largely irrelevant to levels of life satisfaction, according to Dr David Bartram at the University of Leicester.

But his study of 78 countries spanning four decades — the largest longitudinal research of its kind — punctures that myth, he said.

irrelevant to ～：～とは無関係
levels of life satisfaction：生活満足度
Leicester：レスター（英国中央部にある都市）
longitudinal：縦断的
punctures ～：～に穴をあける

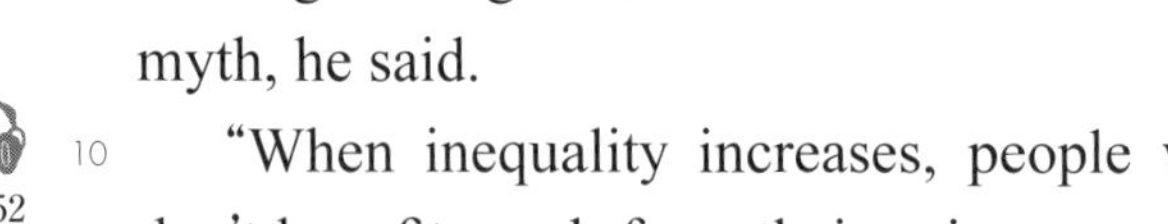
1-52

"When inequality increases, people with high incomes don't benefit much from their gains — many rich people are focused on those who have even more than they do, and they never feel they have enough," Bartram said.

"But people who earn little really suffer from falling further behind — they feel excluded and frustrated by not being able to keep up even with people who receive average incomes."

falling further behind：さらに後れを取ること
excluded：排除された
keep up with ～：～に追いつく

In 1981, as the UK was gripped by a recession, life satisfaction stood at 7.7. But during the economic boom of the 1980s, inequality grew, and the research shows that the happiness figure dropped to 7.4 by 1999.

However, as measures to reduce inequality began to take effect, happiness slowly returned so that by 2018, life satisfaction stood at 7.8.

recession：景気後退、不況
stood at ～：～だった
happiness figure：幸福度
take effect：実施される

1-53

"The data from the UK feeds into a more general finding — in wealthy countries increased inequality has a substantial negative impact on life satisfaction, and inequality has increased in most wealthy countries in recent decades," Bartram said.

feeds into ～：～に反映される
finding：調査結果
has a negative impact on ～：悪影響を及ぼす

This link between higher inequality and lower life satisfaction is repeated elsewhere, Bartram said.

India's life satisfaction declined from 6.7 in 1990 to 5.8 in 2006 as inequality rose. By 2012 it was still lower than in

rose：拡大した

1990, despite the country's prolonged economic boom.

The US and Australia also both saw pronounced falls in life satisfaction, but those countries where inequality had fallen were generally happier, such as Poland, Peru, Mexico and Ukraine, before the Russian invasion.

By James Tapper
*The Guardian News & Media Ltd, April 17, 2022*

fallen：解消された

1-54

## I'm a therapist to the super-rich: they are as miserable as Succession makes out

The television programme Succession, now in its third season, does such a good job of exploring the kinds of toxic excess my clients struggle with that when my wife is watching it I have to leave the room; it just feels like work.

What could possibly be challenging about being a billionaire, you might ask. Well, what would it be like if you couldn't trust those close to you? Or if you looked at any new person in your life with deep suspicion? I hear this from my clients all the time: "What do they want from me?"; or "How are they going to manipulate me?"; or "They are probably only friends with me because of my money."

1-55

Then there are the struggles with purpose — the depression that sets in when you feel like you have no reason to get out of bed. Why bother going to work when the business you have built or inherited runs itself without you now? If all your necessities and much more were covered for the rest of your life — you might struggle with a lack of meaning and ambition too. My clients are often bored with life and too many times this leads to them chasing the next high — chemically or otherwise — to fill that void.

By Clay Cockrell
*The Guardian News & Media Ltd, November 22, 2021*

therapist：セラピスト、（心理）療法士
Succession：相続・継承（問題）《ドラマ名》
makes out：立証する
exploring ～：～を診察する
toxic excess：（心を蝕む）ストレス過剰
what would it be like：どうなるでしょうか
new：初めて会う
with deep suspicion：疑い深い気持ちで
manipulate：操作する
depression：うつ病
Why bother ～：何故わざわざ～するのか
runs itself：稼働する
covered：カバーされる、担保される
ambition：野心
bored with life：人生に飽き飽きする
leads to ～：～に繋がる
void：空虚

## Exercises

### Multiple Choice

次の１～５の英文を完成させるために、ａ～ｄの中から最も適切なものを１つ選びなさい。

**1.** Tapper focuses on ________________ as a factor that can decrease social happiness.

- **a.** equality
- **b.** inequality
- **c.** economic decline
- **d.** economic expansion

**2.** Tapper says that during economic booms ________________ seem to increase.

- **a.** feelings of hope
- **b.** feelings of dissatisfaction
- **c.** feelings of happiness
- **d.** feelings of loneliness

**3.** ________________ is used as an example of satisfaction decreasing.

- **a.** Peru
- **b.** Mexico
- **c.** Ukraine
- **d.** the United Kingdom

**4.** According to the therapist, many rich people get depressed

- **a.** after their friends lose money.
- **b.** if the business they inherit is too challenging.
- **c.** because they stay in bed all day.
- **d.** when all their life's necessities are assured.

**5.** The therapist's clients worry that their friends only want

- **a.** their money.
- **b.** their luck.
- **c.** their house.
- **d.** their happiness.

## True or False

本文の内容に合致するものにT（True)、合致しないものにF（False）をつけなさい。

(　　) **1.** Before the Russian invasion, Ukrainians generally got happier as inequality decreased.

(　　) **2.** It used to be thought that social equality had little influence on happiness.

(　　) **3.** Wealthy people often compare themselves to people who are even richer than them.

(　　) **4.** Many of the therapist's clients turn to drugs because of boredom.

(　　) **5.** Billionaires may question whether they can trust the people close to them.

## Vocabulary

次の１～８は、「通貨」に関する英文です。下の語群の中から最も適切な語を１つ選び、（　）内に記入しなさい。

**1.** The (　　　) is the name of money used formerly in Italy and currently in Turkey.

**2.** One (　　　) dollar is worth more than one New Zealand (　　　).

**3.** Before adopting (　　　) the Irish used pounds and the (　　　) used francs.

**4.** There are 100 centavos in one Brazilian (　　　).

**5.** Danes, Norwegians and Swedes all use a version of the (　　　).

**6.** In both North and South (　　　) the currency is called the (　　　).

**7.** The (　　　) refers to an old British coin and also to money used by Kenyans now.

**8.** Argentinians, Mexicans and Filipinos all call their currency the (　　　).

| | | | | | |
|---|---|---|---|---|---|
| Australian | dollar | euros | French | Korea | krone |
| lira | peso | real | shilling | won | |

Unit **10**

# ●マクロン大統領　ルペンに競り勝ち再選し仏統一を誓う

2022年、フランス大統領選挙で大苦戦の末、現職マクロン氏が再選されるが、国民の「分断」修復は？
AP／アフロ

## *Before you read*

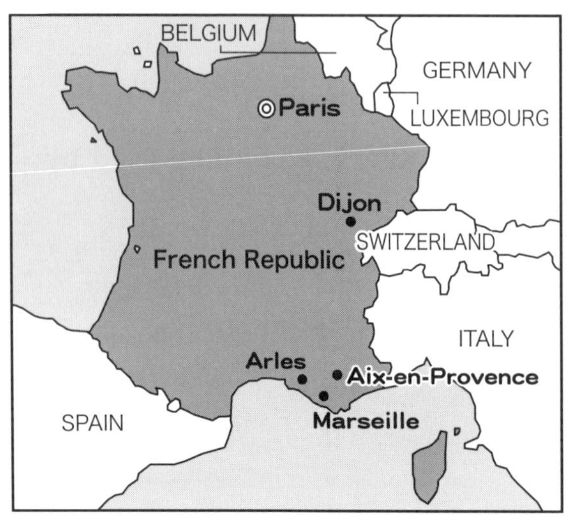


French Republic
フランス共和国

面積　551,500km²（日本の約1.5倍）
人口　67,060,000人
首都　パリ
公用語　フランス語
宗教　カトリック　62%／プロテスタント　2%
　　　イスラム教　6%／ユダヤ教　1%
　　　無宗教　29%
識字率　99%
政体　共和制
GDP　2兆8,400億ドル（世界5位）
　　　1人当たりのGDP　38,625USドル（世界23位）
通貨　ユーロ

## Words and Phrases

次の１～５の語句の説明として最も近いものをａ～ｅから１つ選び、(　) 内に記入しなさい。

**1.** vow (　)
**2.** riven (　)
**3.** abstention (　)
**4.** shake off (　)
**5.** Eurosceptic (　)

**a.** distance oneself from
**b.** doubting the value of the EU
**c.** promise
**d.** split
**e.** choice not to vote or get involved

## Summary

次の英文は記事の要約です。下の語群から最も適切な語を１つ選び、(　) 内に記入しなさい。

1-56 Emmanuel Macron won re-election, which is somewhat (　　) for a French president. But his (　　) of victory against Marine Le Penn was less than when he faced her five years ago. He (　　) that many people voted against her (　　) politics rather than for his own policies. France remains deeply (　　), and he now has to try to unite the people.

acknowledges　divided　margin　rightist　unusual

フランス大統領選挙の第１回投票が、2022年４月10日に行われた。12人が立候補し、現職のマクロン氏が27.84%、極右政党「国民連合」のルペン氏23.15%、急進左派のジャンリュック・メラション氏21.95%の得票率だった。上位２名が４月24日の決選投票に進んだ。マクロン氏は、高学歴、高所得者の多いパリ、リヨン、ボルドーなどの都市部で票を獲得した。一方ルペン氏は、移民や難民の玄関口の地中海沿岸、炭鉱の閉山や重工業の衰退で景気が低迷する北東部で高い支持を集めた。

エマニュエル・マクロンは、1977年に生まれ、国立行政学院（ENA）を卒業後、投資銀行で企業の合併や買収を担当した。2017年39歳の若さで大統領に就任した。EU の統合深化や NATO への拡大を呼びかけ、対ロシア制裁も取りまとめるなど、危機対応に奔走した。マリーヌ・ルペン氏は、1968年に生まれ、パリ第２大学を卒業し、弁護士資格を取得した。物価高騰に苦しむ低・中所得層にエネルギー関連の減税を訴え、支持を拡大した。2017年大統領選では、マクロンがルペンに33.90%の差をつけて圧勝した。

2022年４月24日決戦投票が行われ、マクロン氏が58.54%、ルペン氏41.46%の得票率だった。17.08%の差でルペン氏を破り、マクロン氏が再選を決めた。この再選は、2002年のシラク氏以来20年振りとなった。リヨン政治学院のバコ教授は、今回の選挙は、「マクロン氏は極右を拒絶する国民から支持を得て、ルペン氏はマクロン氏を拒絶する国民から支持を得ている」と述べている。

## Reading

1-57

# Victorious Macron vows to unite France after fending off Le Pen threat

The pro-European centrist Emmanuel Macron has vowed to unite a divided France after winning a second term as French president in a decisive victory against the far-right's Marine Le Pen, who nonetheless won more than 13 million votes in a historic high for her anti-immigration party.

Macron became the first French leader to win re-election for 20 years, scoring 58.54% to Le Pen's 41.46%.

"I know that a number of French people have voted for me today, not to support my ideas but to stop the ideas of the far right," he said and called on supporters to be "kind and respectful" to others, because the country was riven by "so much doubt, so much division".

1-58

Macron beat Le Pen with a lower margin than the 66% he won against her in 2017. Turnout was also lower than five years ago, with abstention estimated at a record 28%.

Le Pen succeeded in delivering the far right its biggest-ever score in a French presidential election, after campaigning on the cost of living crisis, and promising a ban on the Muslim headscarf in public places as well as nationalist measures to give priority to native-French people over others for jobs, housing, benefits and healthcare — policies Macron had criticised as "racist" and "divisive".

Macron's victory was swiftly welcomed by EU leaders after a campaign the French president had described in its final days as a "battle for Europe" against the Eurosceptic Le Pen.

1-59

During a frantic final two weeks' campaigning, Macron had travelled to town squares across France to shake off what he felt was the unjustly persistent tag of a being an aloof "president of the rich". He had promised to dedicate the next five years to restoring France to full employment, arguing that

fending off ～：～をかわす
pro-European：親ヨーロッパの
centrist：中道派、穏健派
far-right：極右
anti-immigration：反移民を政策に掲げる
called on ～ to …：～に…するよう呼び掛けた
doubt：疑念、不信
margin：差、開き
Turnout：投票者数
abstention：棄権
cost of living：生活費
Muslim：イスラム教徒の
nationalist：民族主義的
give priority to ～：～を優先する
benefits：給付金
Eurosceptic：欧州懐疑論者の
dedicate ～ to …：～を…に捧げる

his policies such as loosening French labour laws had already succeeded in creating jobs and that he would definitively put an end to the country's decades of mass unemployment.

- loosening 〜：〜を緩和する

1-60

But although Macron has promised his own swift new package of laws to address the cost of living crisis and tempered his time frame for raising the retirement age, he ultimately focused far less on his own manifesto in the final days and more on stopping what he called the "unthinkable": the far-right, anti-immigration Le Pen taking the helm in France, the eurozone's second biggest economy and a nuclear power.

- package of laws：一括法案
- address 〜：〜に対処する
- manifesto：公約
- nuclear power：核兵器保有国

1-61

Macron had framed the choice between himself and Le Pen as "a referendum on Europe, ecology and secularism" and said the far-right leader's demands for EU treaty change would have led to France being pushed out of the bloc. He called her a "climate sceptic" and said her plan to ban the Muslim headscarf from all public places, including the street, would breach the French constitution and religious liberties, and spark "a civil war".

- referendum：国民投票
- secularism：世俗主義
- "climate sceptic"：「気候変動懐疑論者」《気象学者の研究結果を受け入れない人》
- breach 〜：〜に違反する
- constitution：憲法
- spark 〜：〜の口火となる

Macron accused Le Pen of being financially "dependent" on Vladimir Putin's Russia after she took out a Russian loan for her party in 2014, and said her ties to the Kremlin meant she would have been a dangerous choice at the time of war in Ukraine.

- accused 〜 of …：…したと〜を非難した
- took out a Russian loan：ロシアの融資を受けた
- ties to 〜：〜との関係
- Kremlin：ロシア政府《クレムリンは宮殿名》
- meant 〜：そのことは（主語の結果として）〜になった

By Jon Henley
*The Guardian News & Media Ltd, April 25, 2022.*

## *Exercises*

### Multiple Choice

次の１～５の英文を完成させるために、ａ～ｄの中から最も適切なものを１つ選びなさい。

**1.** Emmanuel Macron became the

**a.** only French president to return after being out of power for twenty years.
**b.** only Frenchman to have won two presidential elections in a row.
**c.** first French leader to serve twenty years continuously in office.
**d.** first French leader to win re-election in the last twenty years.

**2.** Macron's margin of victory over Le Pen was

**a.** larger than in their previous contest.
**b.** smaller than in 2017.
**c.** nearly 59% this time.
**d.** a record 28%.

**3.** Some French people seem to have voted for Macron

**a.** because of his anti-religious policies.
**b.** despite Le Pen's leftist politics.
**c.** because of Le Pen's rightist politics.
**d.** despite his dependence on Vladimir Putin.

**4.** EU leaders acclaimed Macron's victory because of Le Pen's

**a.** decision to exchange euros for pounds.
**b.** extreme pro-EU stance.
**c.** lack of support for the European Union.
**d.** plans to close down the eurozone's nuclear plants.

**5.** Macron has promised to ____________________ France.

**a.** divide a united
**b.** end the civil war in
**c.** ban headscarves in
**d.** unite a divided

## True or False

本文の内容に合致するものにT（True)、合致しないものにF（False）をつけなさい。

( ) **1.** In 2014, Le Pen's party became financially reliant on the Kremlin.

( ) **2.** Macron had vowed to end the cost of living crisis and unemployment.

( ) **3.** Marine Le Pen won more than thirty million votes.

( ) **4.** Macron succeeded because of overwhelming support for his policies.

( ) **5.** Macron referred to the war in Ukraine during his campaign.

## Vocabulary

次の英文は、the New York Timesに掲載された*Macron and Le Pen spar in an increasingly divided France*『マクロンとルペンは、ますます分裂するフランスで火花を散らしている』の記事の一部です。下の語群から最も適切な語を１つ選び、（ ）内に記入しなさい。

In the course of a visit this past week to Saint-Denis, north of Paris, where the ( ) rate is about twice the national average, President Emmanuel Macron donned boxing gloves for a moment to ( ) with a local. "Go on, hit me," the young man said, "show me what you got!"

It was a stop late in a long campaign during which Mr. Macron, distracted by his ( ) Russia diplomacy, had largely ignored parts of France affected by high immigration, ( ) and hardship — and had seldom shown a real concern for the ( ) difficulties that rising inflation and gas ( ) have brought.

Marine Le Pen, the far-right candidate who has brought her ( ) movement closer to power than at any time in the history of the Fifth Republic, focused on precisely these issues, to considerable effect. On Sunday, a bruising ( ) battle between Ms. Le Pen and Mr. Macron will come to a head as the French choose their president for a five-year term.

| anti-immigrant | economic | fruitless | gloves-off |
|---|---|---|---|
| poverty | prices | spar | unemployment |

# Unit 11

## ●仕事の未来：流行りの職場５選

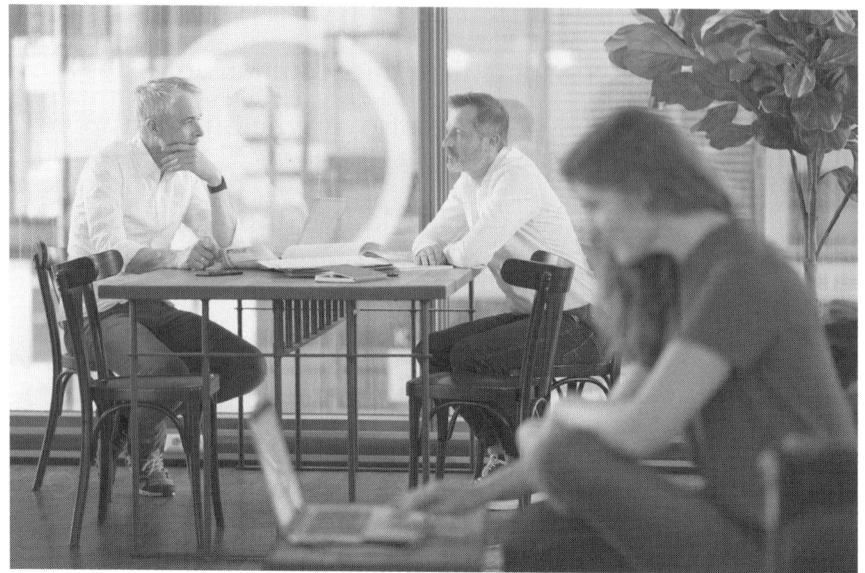

男性起業家たちが話をしている傍らでパソコンを使い「会社」の仕事をする女性会社員
WESTEND61／アフロ

## Before you read

### Questions

1. Do you think it is better to work from home or at a workplace?
   自宅で仕事をするか、職場で仕事をするか、どちらがいいと思いますか？

2. Do you think AI is creating more jobs than it destroys?
   AI は壊すよりも多くの雇用を生み出していると思いますか？

## Words and Phrases

次の１～５の語句の説明として最も近いものをａ～ｅから１つ選び、(　　) 内に記入しなさい。

| | | | |
|---|---|---|---|
| **1.** align with | (　　) | **a.** | stability or ability to keep going |
| **2.** hot-desking | (　　) | **b.** | allocating work-stations on a rotating basis |
| **3.** resilience | (　　) | **c.** | observe or supervise |
| **4.** intrusive | (　　) | **d.** | conform to |
| **5.** oversee | (　　) | **e.** | interfering |

## Summary

次の英文は記事の要約です。下の語群から最も適切な語を１つ選び、(　　) 内に記入しなさい。

1-62 Work (　　　) continue to change. More people will have a choice about where to work, many (　　　) between visiting offices and working remotely. A.I. will become an important tool, while taking (　　　) some jobs entirely. Employers will also have to pay more attention to their workers' physical and (　　　) health. And so employees may find themselves being (　　　) more closely.

| alternating | financial | monitored | over | practices |
|---|---|---|---|---|

Hybrid working（ハイブリッド・ワーク）とは、リモート勤務とオフィス勤務を柔軟に組み合わせた働き方のことを指す。最近は、オフィスか自宅かだけでなく、シェアオフィスやコーワーキングスペースといった働く場が増えている。ハイブリッド・ワークは新しいワークスタイルとして認知されつつあり、今後主流になると考えられている。このハイブリッド・ワークを進めることにより、良い点、不利な点、さらに今後の課題もあると思われる。

まず良い点としては、会社勤務か自宅勤務を自由に選べるため、最適な環境で仕事ができ、生産性の向上が期待できるし、従業員の満足度も上がる。結果的に優秀な人材を確保できる。しかし、不利な点は、家だと会社ほど集中できないし、社内しかできない仕事もある。従来のコミュニケーション方法では意思疎通がしづらくなる。従業員が様々な場所で働いているため、勤怠管理が難しくなり、もともと予定していなかった業務や緊急の会議にも対応しにくくなる。さらに、職場に対しての帰属意識が薄れていく可能性もある。

それでは、ハイブリッド・ワークを向上させるために、従来の固定席を廃止して、スペースをもっと自由に使えるようなオフィス環境の整備が必要だ。オフィスの PC をテレワーク用 PC から遠隔操作する方式にしたり、オフィス PC を持ち帰る事のできる方式を取り入れたり、また、Web 会議システムや勤怠管理システムの導入なども必要だ。さらに、業務を円滑に行うため、ハイブリッド・ワーク導入後もコミュニケーションを意識的に取ることが大切だ。

## Reading

1-63

# Future Of Work: The 5 Biggest Workplace Trends In 2022

### Hybrid working

When it comes to where we work, there will continue to be three main models — centralized workplaces, decentralized remote organizations, and the hybrid "best of both worlds" approach. What's likely to change in 2022 is that it's more likely that we, as workers, will have the choice rather than being forced to align with whatever model your organization has chosen out of necessity.

Hybrid structures will range from companies maintaining permanent centralized offices with hot-desking to accommodate the fact that staff will more frequently work remotely, to doing away with offices entirely and relying on co-working spaces and serviced meeting rooms to support the needs of a primarily remote workforce.

1-64

### AI-augmented workforce

The World Economic Forum predicts that AI and automation will lead to the creation of 97 million new jobs by 2025. However, people working in many existing jobs will also find their roles changing, as they are increasingly expected to augment their own abilities with AI technology. Initially, this AI will primarily be used to automate repetitive elements of their day-to-day roles and allow workers to focus on areas that require a more human touch — creativity, imagination, high-level strategy, or emotional intelligence, for example. Some examples include lawyers who will use technology that cuts down the amount of time spent reviewing case histories in order to find precedents, and doctors who will have computer vision capabilities to help them analyze medical records and scans to help them diagnose illness in patients.

1-65

### Staffing for resilience

Pre-pandemic, the priority was generally to have been

When it comes to ～：～に関しては
decentralized：分散型の
align with ～：～に合わせる
out of necessity：必要に応じて
hot-desking：ホットデスキング《職場で複数の人たちが１つの机やコンピュータなどを共有するシステム》
doing away with ～：～を廃止する
co-working：コワーキング《異なる企業に属する人たちが経費削減のため、１つの事務スペースを共有しながら仕事をすること》
AI-augmented：AI（人工知能）で強化された
World Economic Forum：世界経済フォーラム《ダボスでの賢人会議》
touch：特徴
emotional intelligence：感情的知性《人間関係を上手く維持する能力》
case histories：事例
computer vision：コンピュータ画像
diagnose ～：～を診断する
Staffing：人員配置
resilience：レジリエンス、回復力
generally to have been：一般的には昔からずっとそうだが《挿入と考える》

to hire staff that would create efficient organizations. Mid and post-pandemic, the emphasis has shifted firmly in the direction of resilience.

This certainly encompasses another sub-trend, which is that employers are coming to understand the critical importance of building employee healthcare and wellbeing (including mental health) strategies into their game plan. Many are now trying to take more responsibility for helping their workforce maintain physical, mental, and financial wellbeing. A challenge here that companies will come up against in 2022 is finding ways to do this that hit objectives without being overly intrusive or invasive of employees' privacy and personal lives.

1-66

## Less focus on roles, more focus on skills

Skills are critical because they address core business challenges, with the competencies needed in a workforce to overcome those challenges. Roles, on the other hand, describe the way individual members of a workforce relate to an overall organizational structure or hierarchy. By focussing on skills, businesses address the fact that solving problems and answering their core business questions is the key to driving innovation and success within information-age enterprises.

1-67

## Employee monitoring and analytics

Controversial though it may be, research shows that employers are increasingly investing in technology designed to monitor and track the behavior of their employees in order to drive efficiency. Platforms such as Aware that allow businesses to monitor behavior across email and tools such as Slack in order to measure productivity, are being seen as particularly useful by managers overseeing remote workforces.

By Bernard Marr
*Forbes, November 23, 2021*

game plan：作戦、行動計画
challenge：課題
come up against：～に直面する
address ～：～に対処する
competencies：能力
hierarchy：階層
driving ～：～を推進する
monitoring：監視
Controversial though it may be：物議を醸すかも知れませんが
Platforms：プラットフォーム、（情報配信やビジネスを行うための）基盤
tools：ツール《プログラムを作るときなどに使われる、小規模なユーティリティ・プログラム》
Slack：《メッセージ・プログラムの一種》
*Forbes*：フォーブス《米国経済誌》

## Exercises

### Multiple Choice

次の１～５の英文を完成させるために、a～dの中から最も適切なものを１つ選びなさい。

**1.** Offices with "hot-desking"

**a.** have done away with permanent facilities.
**b.** provide working spaces in remote locations.
**c.** assume that only some employees come in on some days.
**d.** guarantee enough desks for all employees.

**2.** It is predicted that AI will

**a.** create some new jobs and change some existing jobs.
**b.** replace doctors and lawyers.
**c.** mainly perform tasks requiring creativity.
**d.** only help people doing boring or repetitive work.

**3.** Post-pandemic, employers will focus on supporting employees'

**a.** privacy.
**b.** mental and physical health.
**c.** personalities.
**d.** sense of responsibility.

**4.** Skills are described as more task-oriented, while roles seem to be more

**a.** happiness-oriented.
**b.** profit-oriented.
**c.** organization-oriented.
**d.** competency-oriented.

**5.** The increase in remote work means employers are

**a.** investing in technology to monitor employees.
**b.** being monitored more by their employees.
**c.** reluctant to monitor employees out of concern for their privacy.
**d.** unable to monitor employees outside the office.

## True or False

本文の内容に合致するものにＴ（True）、合致しないものにＦ（False）をつけなさい。

( ) **1.** Tools such as Aware are used by businesses to send emails to employees.

( ) **2.** Employers will focus on roles more than on skills.

( ) **3.** Employers are becoming more interested in employees' healthcare and wellbeing.

( ) **4.** Workers are increasingly expected to enhance their abilities with AI technology.

( ) **5.** The article suggests that work patterns will become less varied.

## Vocabulary

次の１～８は、「働く」に関する英文です。日本文に合わせて、適切な語を下の語群から１つ選び、（　）内に記入しなさい。

**1.** なりふり構わず働くということは、一生懸命働くことだ。
If you work like a ( ), you work very hard.

**2.** 骨身を惜しまず働くということは、特に長時間働くということだ。
If you work your ( ) to the bone, you work extremely hard, especially, for a long time.

**3.** 死ぬまで働くというのはあまり疲れていてもう働くことが出来ないまで働くことだ。
If you work till you ( ), you work until you are so tired that you cannot work any more.

**4.** あなたは全く仕事中毒人間だ。仕事があなたの全人生だ。
You're a complete ( ) — your job is your whole life.

**5.** "よく遊び、よく学べ" ということは勉強ばかりしているとつまらない人になるという意味だ。
"All work and no ( ) makes Jack a dull boy" means that someone who works all of the time will become boring and uninteresting.

**6.** 会社は、我々にテレワークをするように促している。
Our company encourages us to work ( ).

**7.** 好きなところで働くフリーランスの在宅勤務者だ。
He is a freelance ( ) who works wherever he wants.

**8.** 学生ローン返済のため20年間働く必要がある。
I need twenty years to work ( ) their student loans.

| dog | drop | fingers | off |
|---|---|---|---|
| play | remotely | telecommuter | workaholic |

Unit **12**

# ●マッチング・アプリで実際のデートは？

マッチングアプリのイメージ。あなたに最適な相手が見つかるかも？

イメージマート

## *Before you read*

### Questions

**1.** What do you think the article will be about?

この記事は何の話題についてだと思いますか？

**2.** What do you know about matching apps?

マッチング・アプリについて何か知っていますか？

## Words and Phrases

次の１～５の語の説明として最も近いものをａ～ｅから１つ選び、(　　) 内に記入しなさい。

| | | | |
|---|---|---|---|
| **1.** recurring | (　　) | **a.** develop |
| **2.** evolve | (　　) | **b.** threateningly |
| **3.** menacingly | (　　) | **c.** large or seeking to impress |
| **4.** convincingly | (　　) | **d.** frequently arising |
| **5.** grandiose | (　　) | **e.** persuasively |

## Summary

次の英文は記事の要約です。下の語群から最も適切な語を１つ選び、(　　) 内に記入しなさい。

1-68

The author of a new book claims that the internet has made us feel that (　　　) is no longer a part of (　　　) social behavior. People do things (　　　) that they would not do in (　　　). Some, for example, stop replying to someone's messages yet continue to like their posts. Many try to keep their social contacts and dating contacts completely (　　　).

dating　　general　　online　　person　　separate

マッチング・アプリは、モバイル・アプリケーションを介して提供されるオンライン恋愛サービスのことで、多くの場合、スマートフォンのGPS機能、携帯性、デジタル・フォト・ギャラリーやモバイル・ウォレットへの簡易なアクセスを利用して、インターネット上の出会いを円滑にさせている。これらのアプリは、インターネット上で知り合った相手とチャットしたり、会合したりする、従来のオンライン恋愛サービスのプロセスを簡素化し、迅速化することができる。

マッチング・アプリの使用には、利点も欠点もある。多くのアプリは、マッチングのための性格検査や計算法や処理法のアルゴリズムを使ってユーザーをマッチングさせる。ユーザーが好みの候補者とマッチングする可能性が高まる。興味が持てない候補者とはマッチングしないことを選択するだけで、選択肢を絞り込むことができる。候補者とはチャットして人柄を知ることができ、時間、費用、およびリスクを軽減させる。しかし、欠点としては選択肢が多いとユーザーは迷い、完璧な候補者を探すのにかなりの時間がかかってしまう可能性がある。さらに、導入されているアルゴリズムとマッチング・システムは、正確であるとは限らない。二人の性格を完全に一致させることができる完璧なシステムはない。オンラインでのコミュニケーションには、物理的な側面も欠けている。メールのやりとりだけでは、多くのことを知ることができない。オンライン恋愛は恋愛を非常に表面的なものにしている。

## Reading

1-69

# Apps promised a sexual revolution but they have just made dating weird

One feature of online dating that makes it a recurring pub-discussion topic among my friends is the propensity for the people involved to do strange things. A whole new spectrum of dating behaviour has evolved on “the apps”. Habits that, while now common, are still odd things to do.

Someone might seem very interested but then “ghost” or “orbit” (which means they stop replying to messages but still engage with your social media content, liking your posts and photos); or tell obvious but seemingly unnecessary lies; another person might read “the riot act” on a first date, sternly laying down their terms for how the relationship should progress; and there are endless stories about dates reacting bizarrely, even menacingly, if rejected.

1-70

One I heard recently was about a man my friend met on an app. When she told him she didn’t want to see him again he went through a phase of sending her pictures from her own social media accounts, platforms they had never interacted on, as if to say: “I’ve got my eye on you.” But most of it is not really threatening, just plain strange. I haven’t dated in a little while but (and there is no way to say this without sounding like I’m 90) I had my Tinder phase, and I remember the strangeness well. One man I matched with spent months sending me puns and jokes based on the TV show How Clean is Your House?

1-71

The apps have created a dating landscape that is largely divorced from our normal social ecosystem of friends and acquaintances — people whose opinions we care about, who might judge us for ghosting someone or consistently treating dates badly. There are rarely wider social consequences for anything we do when we date strangers we meet online, and so we are free to get up to all sorts.

Apps：アプリケーション（応用）ソフト
weird：変な、奇妙な
propensity：傾向
for ～ to …：～が…する《propensity に係る》
evolved on ～：～で進化した
“ghost”：「ゴースト」《付き合いを急に止めて一切連絡しないこと》
“orbit”：「オービット」《周りをうろつく》
engage with ～：～と関わる
liking ～：～を高く評価する
posts：投稿
riot act：暴動行為
laying down ～：～を規定する
terms for ～：～についての条件
went through ～：～を経た、通過した
interacted：交流した
Tinder：ティンダー《マッチングアプリの一つ：メッセージを交換する前に両者のユーザーがお互いを好きでなければならない「ダブル・オプ・トレイン」システムを使用》
How Clean is Your House?：「どう、きれいになったでしょ」《ゴミ部屋（屋敷）をプロの清掃人がきれいにする英国の娯楽番組》
divorced from ～：～から絶縁された
ecosystem：生態系
consequences：影響
get up to ～：～（好ましくないこと）を行う

1-72

A new book, The New Laws of Love: Online Dating and the Privatization of Intimacy, by Marie Bergström, a sociologist and researcher who works at the National Institute of Demographic Studies in France, explores this premise. She argues convincingly that the growing popularity of online dating has increasingly removed it from the public sphere, turning it into an entirely "domestic and individual practice". She terms this the "privatisation of intimacy".

The book has a refreshing lack of hysteria about the impact the internet has had on our sex lives, and no grandiose declarations about the state of love today. Bergström's interviews with young people, who conduct almost their entire dating life online, illuminate a culture where dating is often so detached from their wider social network that the idea of mixing the two evokes panic.

1-73

One of her interviewees, a 22-year-old, admits she won't even match with people on apps whom she shares contacts with. "Even at the relationship level, I don't know if it's healthy to have so many friends in common," she says. Another 22-year-old balks at the idea of treating a regular, non-dating social media website as a place where you might find a partner: "These are people you already know!" he exclaims.

By Rachel Connolly
*The Guardian News & Media Ltd, December 28, 2021*

Privatization：私物化
Intimacy：親密さ
Demographic：人口学の
premise：前提
terms ～ …：～を…と呼ぶ
declarations：宣言
detached：切り離された
the two：この二つのデート方法
evokes ～：～を呼び起こす
in common：共通の
balks at ～：～にためらう、尻込みする

## Exercises

### Multiple Choice

次の１の英文の質問に答え、２～５の英文を完成させるために、a～dの中から最も適切なものを１つ選びなさい。

**1.** What does "orbit" mean in this article?

**a.** The way small bodies move around large bodies.
**b.** The circling of the moon around the earth.
**c.** Circling around nearby without entering a conversation.
**d.** Blocking people so that they cannot contact you online.

**2.** Matching apps give us the chance to ____________________ immediately.

**a.** have an online date with someone
**b.** check who our friends are dating
**c.** meet someone at a bar or restaurant
**d.** travel together

**3.** Marie Bergström argues that the online shift in dating has changed it

**a.** from an individual to a group practice.
**b.** from a private to a public practice.
**c.** from a romantic to a financial activity.
**d.** from a partly public to a largely private activity.

**4.** This change seems ____________________ Bergström.

**a.** to worry
**b.** not to shock
**c.** to frustrate
**d.** not to interest

**5.** Young people appear to prefer dating other people who

**a.** do not know their friends.
**b.** they have known since they were young.
**c.** they can introduce easily to their friends.
**d.** do not use online apps.

## True or False

本文の内容に合致するものにT（True）、合致しないものにF（False）をつけなさい。

(　　) **1.** "The New Laws of Love: Online Dating and the Privatization of Intimacy" is written by Marie Bergström.

(　　) **2.** People seem to find it easier to treat others badly online if they think their friends cannot see their behavior.

(　　) **3.** Many people do things online that they would not do in person.

(　　) **4.** Bergström once used to work at the National Institute of Demographic Studies in France.

(　　) **5.** Some continue to like photos and posts even after they stop exchanging messages.

## Vocabulary

次の１～８は、AI artificial intelligence に関する語句です。下のａ～ｈの説明文の中から最も適切なものを１つ選び、(　　) 内に記入しなさい。

**1.** app (　　)
**2.** AlphaGo (　　)
**3.** AI (　　)
**4.** algorithm (　　)
**5.** Smartphone (　　)
**6.** Tablet (　　)
**7.** drone (　　)
**8.** chatbot (　　)

**a.** a mobile phone that can be used as a small computer and that connects to the internet
**b.** a shortening of the term "application software"
**c.** personal mobile computer which is used by tapping with a finger on a touch screen
**d.** the first computer program to defeat a professional human GO player
**e.** the ability of a computer program to think and learn, and also a field of study which tries to make computer smart
**f.** an aircraft without a pilot that is controlled by someone on the ground
**g.** a pattern that a computer follows to complete a task
**h.** a robot that can respond to spoken or written questions from people

Unit **13**

# ●中国　離婚率と結婚率低下

婚姻登録所で結婚証明書を手に、記念写真する若い中国人夫婦　　AFP ／ WAA

## *Before you read*

People's Republic of China
中華人民共和国

面積　9,634,057km²（日本の約25倍）（世界４位）
人口　1,433,784,000人（世界１位）
首都　北京／**最大都市**　上海
公用語　中国語
識字率　95.9%
民族　漢族　11億7,000万～12億人（90%～92%）
　55の少数民族８%
　チワン族（1,600万人）満族（1,000万人）
　回族（900万人）ミャオ族（800万人）
　ウイグル族・イ族（各700万人）ブイ族（300万人）
宗教　宗教信者　１億人　0.08%／仏教　6.2%
　キリスト教　2.3%／道教・無宗教　87.4%
　イスラム教　1.7%
GDP　13兆3,680億ドル（世界２位）
　１人当たりのGDP　9,580ドル（世界72位）
通貨　元
政体　一党独裁制の社会主義共和国

## Words and Phrases

次の１～５の語句の説明として最も近いものをａ～ｅから１つ選び、(　　) 内に記入しなさい。

| | | | |
|---|---|---|---|
| **1.** undergo | (　　) | **a.** greet |
| **2.** hail | (　　) | **b.** requirement |
| **3.** manageable | (　　) | **c.** lasting for tens of years |
| **4.** prerequisite | (　　) | **d.** be subjected to |
| **5.** decades-old | (　　) | **e.** able to cope with |

## Summary

次の英文は記事の要約です。下の語群から最も適切な語を１つ選び、(　　) 内に記入しなさい。

1-74

(　　　　) Chinese are marrying or having children. Worried about an impending population (　　　　), the government is emphasizing family values. Couples wanting to divorce must now (　　　　) for 30 days. This requirement does seem to have (　　　　) the divorce rate. But the marriage rate is continuing to fall, with many people (　　　　) pressure from their families to get married.

drop　　fewer　　resisting　　slowed　　wait

中国は、1979年に「一人っ子政策」を導入し、夫婦の子供の数を１人に制限し、２人目から罰金を科したが、2016年に「二人っ子政策」、2021年には「三人っ子政策」を打ち出して、出産奨励に転じた。もし「一人っ子政策」を実施していなかったら、総人口は17億から18億になっていたと言われている。しかし、少子化に歯止めがかからない。国家統計局によると、出生数は、2019年の1465万人、20年1200万人、21年1062万人と毎年減少している。

政府の国家衛生健康委員会は、①20歳から34歳の女性の減少 ②晩婚化が進み、出産意欲も低下 ③出産・子育て・教育コストの高止まりの３点の理由を挙げた。「一人っ子政策」と男子偏重の影響を受け、2021年の20歳から40歳までの結婚適齢期の男女比が108.9対100で明らかに男性の結婚相手が不足している。また意欲的な女性には、仕事と家庭・育児の両立が困難なため、結婚や出産を避ける傾向にある。婚姻件数も2013年には1347万組、以後毎年減少して20年に813万組、21年763万組となり、13年より40%以上も減少している。

中国が「社会主義社会」から「市場経済導入社会」へ変化したため、出産や育児、教育が公的に保障されていたが、現在は個人の負担となった。経済発展の中で競争社会となり、子供の教育、習い事に経済力が問われることとなった。さらに、65歳以上の人口が２億56万人で、総人口14億1260万人の14.2%の割合に拡大し、「高齢化社会」となった。高齢人口の急増は、現役世代や財政の重荷となる。「少子高齢化」は、中国が直面する最大の課題となっている。

## Reading

1-75

# Divorce Is Down in China, but So Are Marriages

Divorce：離婚
So Are ～：～もだ《前文（肯定文）の述部を受ける》

HONG KONG — Faced with a soaring divorce rate, the ruling Communist Party in China introduced a rule last year to keep unhappy marriages together by forcing couples to undergo a 30-day "cooling off" period before finalizing a divorce.

soaring：高騰する
introduced ～：～を導入した

The rule appears to have worked, according to government statistics released this week, which show a steep drop in divorce filings in 2021.

statistics：統計
divorce filings：離婚届

Local officials have hailed the new rule as a success in the country's effort to grow families and curb a demographic crisis threatening China's economy. But the party has a much bigger challenge to reckon with: Fewer and fewer Chinese citizens are getting married in the first place.

curb ～：～を抑える
demographic crisis：人口動態危機
reckon with ～：～を考慮する
in the first place：そもそも

1-76

Along with the decline in the divorce rate, the number of marriage registrations plunged to a 36-year low in 2021. The fall in marriages has contributed to a plummet in birthrates, a worrying sign in China's rapidly graying society and a phenomenon more familiar in countries like Japan and South Korea.

36-year low：36年ぶりの低水準
contributed to ～：～の一因となった
graying society：高齢化する社会

Many young Chinese people say they would prefer not to get married, as a job becomes harder to find, competition more fierce and the cost of living less manageable.

prefer not to ～：～したくない

1-77

"I do not want to get married at all," said Yao Xing, a 32-year-old bachelor who lives in the city of Dandong, near China's border with North Korea. His parents are pressuring him to get married and have children, but Mr. Yao said his job buying and selling kitchenware had made it hard to keep a steady income, which he sees as a prerequisite to marriage. Besides, he added, many women don't want to get married anyway.

bachelor：独身男性
Dandong：丹東
prerequisite to ～：～に対する前提条件

"I think more and more people around me don't want to get married, and the divorce rate and marriage rate in China have dropped significantly, which I think is an irreversible trend," Mr. Yao said.

1-78

Rising gender inequality at work and at home has caused many women to think twice about marriage as well. Better educated and more financially independent than their mothers, younger women have watched as their economic position has changed while society's view of them has not.

The couples who do get married in China often prefer not to have children, citing worries about the rising cost of education and the burden of taking care of aging parents while also having young children. Some are delaying getting married, choosing instead to live together without the ceremony and, often, without the children.

1-79

"The relatively lower marriage rates coupled with rising divorce rates might signal the deinstitutionalization of marriage, which means more people might choose cohabitation over marriage," said Ye Liu, a senior lecturer in the department of international development at King's College London.

Fearful of the day when the population might begin to shrink, the Chinese government has spent years introducing policies to encourage marriage and having children. It has revised strict family planning rules twice in the last decade, first by ending a decades-old "one child" policy in 2015, and later by allowing married couples to have three children.

By Alexandra Stevenson
*The New York Times, March 23, 2022*

irreversible：不可逆的な
think twice：考え直す
watches as 〜：〜するのを見てきた
citing 〜：〜を理由に挙げる
burden：負担
deinstitutionalization：非制度化
choose 〜 over …：…より〜の方を選ぶ
cohabitation：同棲、共同生活
department：学部、学科
King's College London：《ロンドン大学のカレッジの一つ》
shrink：縮小、減少
revised 〜：〜を改訂した

## Exercises

### Multiple Choice

次の１～５の英文を完成させるために、ａ～ｄの中から最も適切なものを１つ選びなさい。

**1.** The Chinese Communist Party introduced a requirement that couples

**a.** delay marriage in order to reduce the likelihood of divorce later.
**b.** refrain from filing for divorce until they have been married for thirty days.
**c.** experience three weeks of "cooling off" before filing for divorce.
**d.** wait for thirty days before signing divorce papers.

**2.** One reason for birthrates plummeting in China is

**a.** an increase in people delaying their divorce.
**b.** a decrease in the cost of living.
**c.** a decrease in marriages.
**d.** an increase in the age of children.

**3.** Many Chinese couples do not have children because

**a.** schooling is getting costly.
**b.** they may have to care for aging parents.
**c.** they choose to live together without marrying.
**d.** of all of the above reasons.

**4.** Problems that China has include the declining divorce rate and

**a.** arrival of an aging society.
**b.** soaring female education.
**c.** economic growth rate.
**d.** fierce competition for leadership.

**5.** The Chinese government's "one-child" policy

**a.** continues to prevent couples from having children.
**b.** used to allow couples to have up to three children.
**c.** was abandoned when population growth slowed.
**d.** discouraged couples from marrying.

## True or False

本文の内容に合致するものにT（True）、合致しないものにF（False）をつけなさい。

(　　) **1.** The article says that China's population is shrinking.

(　　) **2.** The decline in marriages has contributed to a rise in birthrates.

(　　) **3.** Divorce rates have been falling in China for many years.

(　　) **4.** Falling birthrates used to worry Japan and South Korea more than China.

(　　) **5.** A falling birthrate will lead to a decline in the number of people of working age.

## Vocabulary

次の1～6は、結婚や離婚、少子高齢化に関する社会問題を扱った英文です。日本文に合わせて、下の語群から最も適切な語を1つ選び、（　）内に記入しなさい。

**1.** 結婚したい男性と結婚する気のない女性が、隣同士で座っている。
A man who wants to (　　　　) and a woman who is not willing to get (　　　　) sit next to each other.

**2.** 我々夫婦は、協議離婚をすることになった。
My husband and I ended up having a (　　　　) by (　　　　).

**3.** 性格の不一致が理由で離婚する夫婦が増えている。
Increasingly more couples are getting (　　　　) on grounds of (　　　　).

**4.** 日本社会が抱える問題に少子高齢化がある。
Problems that Japan has include the (　　　　) birthrate and (　　　　) society.

**5.** 社会保障制度を充実させる必要がある。
The social (　　　　) system should be enhanced.

**6.** 国籍や性別、職業などで人を差別してはいけない。
Do not (　　　　) against people based on nationality, gender or occupation.

| aging | consent | declining | discriminate | divorce |
|---|---|---|---|---|
| divorced | incompatibility | married | marry | security |

Unit 14

# ●カナダでトラック運転手が抗議運動　何故？

新型コロナ感染症を巡り、カナダでトラック運転手たちがワクチン接種義務に抗議する。果たして、その経緯と結末は？　The New York Times ／ Redux ／アフロ

## Before you read

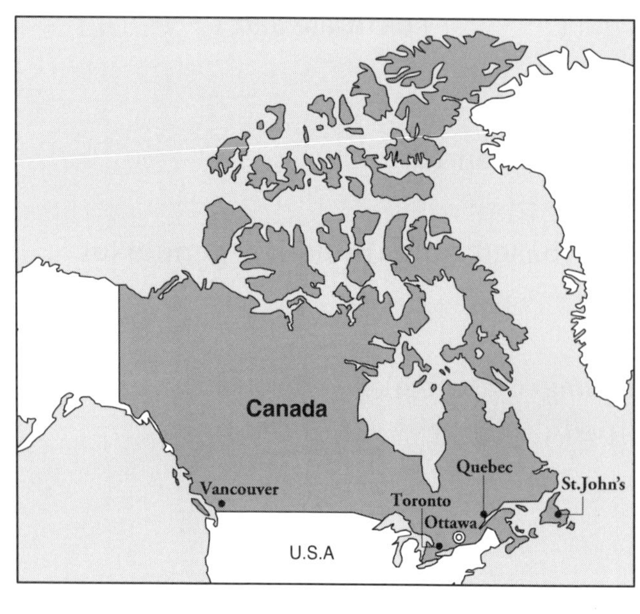


Canada
カナダ

面積　9,984,670km²（世界２位、日本の約26倍）
人口　37,890,000人
公用語　英語、フランス語
識字率　99%
首都　オタワ／**最大都市**　トロント
人種　欧州系白人　76.7%／アジア系　7.6%
　東アジア系　4.8%／先住民族　4.3%
　黒人　2.9%／アラブ系　1.8%／中南米系　1.2%
宗教　キリスト教　77%
　（カトリック　43.2%／プロテスタント　29.2%）
　イスラム教　２%／ユダヤ教　1.1%
　仏教　１%／ヒンドゥ教　１%／無宗教　16.5%
通貨　カナダドル
GDP　１兆9,392億米ドル
　１人当たりのGNI　46,460米ドル
政体　立憲君主制

## Words and Phrases

次の１～５の語句の説明として最も近いものを a ～ e から１つ選び、（　）内に記入しなさい。

**1.** paralyze (　　)
**2.** clog (　　)
**3.** break off (　　)
**4.** en route to (　　)
**5.** fringe (　　)

**a.** cause to stop working or moving
**b.** on the way to
**c.** small group with unusual ideas
**d.** block
**e.** separate

## Summary

次の英文は記事の要約です。下の語群から最も適切な語を１つ選び、（　）内に記入しなさい。

2-01

Many truck drivers are frustrated by pandemic (　　　). In Canada most are (　　　) and law-abiding, yet a small minority led by various groups, including (　　　) and right-wingers, have organized protests. As in several other countries, long lines of trucks have blocked roads and (　　　) chaos. Now the government has started to (　　　) protesters.

anti-vaxxers　　arrest　　caused　　restrictions　　vaccinated

カナダの首都オタワで、2022年１月28日から新型コロナウイルス・ワクチンの接種義務化に対する抗議デモ「自由のトラック集団（Freedom Convoy）」が続き、ジム・ワトソン市長が２月６日に非常事態宣言を発令した。抗議デモ開始以来、国会議事堂周辺の道路はトラックなどの大型車両で塞がれ、学校や市庁舎、図書館、ワクチン接種会場、店舗も閉鎖され、市民は外出できない状況だった。その後、抗議するトラック運転手らが３週間にわたり座り込みデモを続けていたが、警察は２月17日夜にはデモ指導者２人を逮捕し、器物損壊と扇動の罪で訴追した。18日、デモ隊を排除する大規模な作戦を開始、複数のトラックを撤去した。

一部のデモ参加者は、マスクの着用やワクチン接種の義務といった新型コロナウイルス対策が緩和されるまでデモを続けるとしている。デモ参加者と警察との間でこう着状態が続くなか、市内の繁華街はデモの影響で営業を停止し、地元経済に対して大きな金銭的損失を引き起こしていると述べている。このデモは、トラック運転手のワクチン接種義務化に抗議するものというが、カナダトラック同盟によると、ドライバーの大多数がワクチン接種を受けており、多くの抗議参加者は、トラック業界とは関係ないとしている。

## Reading

2-02

# Trucker Protests in Canada: What You Need to Know

For weeks, Canadian protesters fighting vaccine requirements have paralyzed Ottawa and key border crossings, inspired demonstrations around the globe and injected political instability into the stunned top of Canadian government.

On Thursday, Canada's patience had worn thin and the police began arresting protesters, hoping to end weeks of gridlock. On Saturday, the police in Ottawa cleared the thoroughfare in front of the Parliament building, arresting 170 people and removing 46 vehicles.

2-03

"It is high time that these illegal and dangerous activities stop," Prime Minister Justin Trudeau said. Earlier in the week, the protests, which had at first seemed small and disorganized, led him to declare Canada's first national public order emergency in half a century.

The weeks of protests have become one of the most visible, and contagious, eruptions of anti-vaccine anger around the world. Similar caravans have clogged traffic on the streets of Belgium, France, New Zealand and even Finland.

2-04

While truckers initiated the protests on Jan. 22, only a few of them are among a group of self-proclaimed leaders involved in the organizing. Far-right activists and separatists from Western Canada have also seized on the issue to air anti-government grievances, as have former police officers and military veterans who many believe have used their expertise to help organize the occupation.

The far-right People's Party of Canada, which has no seats in the federal Parliament, was strongly represented in the ranks of the Ottawa protesters. One of the key organizers of the so-called Freedom Convoy in Ottawa, Tamara Lich, was previously an official with the Maverick Party, which promotes

requirements：（接種）義務付け

Ottawa：オタワ《カナダの首都》

border crossings：国境検問所

instability：不安定さ

worn thin：堪忍袋の緒が切れた、限界に達した

gridlock：交通渋滞

thoroughfare：大通り

Parliament：国会議事堂

national public order emergency：全国社会秩序緊急事態

self-proclaimed ～：～を自称する

separatists：分離（独立）主義者

seized on ～：～に付け込んだ

air ～：～を公表する、表明する

grievances：苦情、抗議、不満

as ～：同じように～も同様だ

occupation：（道路）占拠

People's Party of Canada：カナダ人民党

represented in ～：～に仲間入りした

ranks：集団

Freedom Convoy：自由トラック集団

Maverick Party：マーベリック党

breaking off Canada's three western Prairie provinces from the rest of the country.

Prairie provinces：プレーリー州《大草原地域の3州（アルバータ州、サスカチュワン州、マニトバ州）を指す》

2-05

Ms. Lich, 47, was among those who were arrested on Thursday, according to a spokeswoman for the protest.

The protests started on Jan. 22 when convoys of trucks departed from British Colombia en route to Ottawa, Canada's capital. The drivers were protesting new federal regulations requiring truckers crossing into Canada from the United States to be vaccinated against the coronavirus.

en route to ～：～に向かう途中で

They reached Ottawa on Jan. 28, and threatened to disrupt the economy and make life miserable for residents until federal officials rolled back pandemic restrictions. They were ambitious, issuing blanket demands for the lifting of all of the country's pandemic restrictions and the dissolving of the Parliament and the removal of Mr. Trudeau from office.

rolled back ～：～を撤回した

lifting：解除

dissolving：解散

2-06

Mr. Trudeau initially dismissed the protesters as a "small fringe minority." He had public backing: About 90 percent of all truckers are vaccinated and a majority of Canadians say they support public health measures intended to slow the spread of the coronavirus.

dismissed ～ as …：～を…として退けた

fringe：非主流派の

But the protesters, despite their small numbers, had outsize impact and their traffic-blocking tactics spread to other Canadian cities, including Toronto, Quebec City and Calgary.

During the first 11 days of the protest in Ottawa, truck horns blasted up to 16 hours a day, and some residents say they have been harassed on the street.

horns：クラクション

blasted：大きく鳴り響いた

harassed：嫌がらせを受けた

By Jason Horowitz

*The New York Times, February 20, 2022*

## Exercises

### Multiple Choice

次の１～５の英文を完成させるために、a～dの中から最も適切なものを１つ選びなさい。

**1.** On January 22 Canadian truckers started protesting against

**a.** vaccine requirements.
**b.** political instability.
**c.** the removal of vehicles.
**d.** gridlock on the roads.

**2.** In Canada, declarations of national public disorder

**a.** are increasing.
**b.** seem to be very unusual.
**c.** happen every 50 years.
**d.** can be illegal and dangerous.

**3.** Tamara Lich seems to have wanted

**a.** the Ottawa protesters to be arrested.
**b.** the protesters to join the Maverick Party.
**c.** the truck protests to stop.
**d.** the three Prairie provinces to separate from the rest of Canada.

**4.** The Canadian truck drivers who were protesting were called the

**a.** Maverick Party.
**b.** People's Party.
**c.** Freedom Convoy.
**d.** Fringe Minority.

**5.** The ____________________ had strong representation among the Ottawa protesters.

**a.** far right
**b.** citizens of Toronto and Calgary
**c.** the truckers of Belgium, France and New Zealand
**d.** victims of the Covid-19 virus

## True or False

本文の内容に合致するものにＴ（True)、合致しないものにＦ（False）をつけなさい。

(　　) **1.** Truck drivers crossing from the United States to Canada are required to be vaccinated against yellow fever.

(　　) **2.** Few truckers are vaccinated as they disagree with this measure against the coronavirus.

(　　) **3.** The far-right People's Party of Canada does not have any seats in the federal Parliament.

(　　) **4.** Protesters have also blocked traffic on the streets of Belgium, Finland, France and New Zealand.

(　　) **5.** The protesters in Ottawa kept blowing horns for more than 15 hours a day.

## Vocabulary

次の１～８は、「Coronavirus」に関する英文です。日本文に合わせて、適当な語を下の語群から１つ選び、(　)内に記入しなさい。

**1.** 特に不要不急の仕事の場合は、できるだけ在宅勤務をお願いします。
The authorities ask that people work from home as much as possible, especially if your work is considered (　　　) and non-urgent.

**2.** 政府は、海外への渡航の自粛をお願いしています。
The government has now asked people here to refrain from travel (　　　).

**3.** 自粛ムードは、経済にも影響している。
The air of (　　　) has also had an effect on the economy.

**4.** 感染拡大で日経平均株価が下落する。
The Nikkei Stock Average goes down as the (　　　) of contagion rises.

**5.** ワクチンの開発に期待が高まっている。
People are raising their expectation for the development of (　　　).

**6.** 政府は、すでに医療従事者にワクチン接種を始めた。
The government has already started (　　　) medical workers.

**7.** 高齢者や基礎疾患のある人を優先にワクチン接種が進められている。
The elderly and people with chronic conditions are (　　　) for receiving a vaccination.

**8.** ２回ワクチン接種を受けた人は、今回で３回目の接種となります。
The people who have been vaccinated twice can now get a (　　　).

| booster | nonessential | overseas | prioritized |
|---|---|---|---|
| self-restraint | spread | vaccinating | vaccines |

Unit **15**

# ●中国との争いで小国のリトアニア・ブランドが排斥される

# ●ニカラグアが台湾との同盟破棄

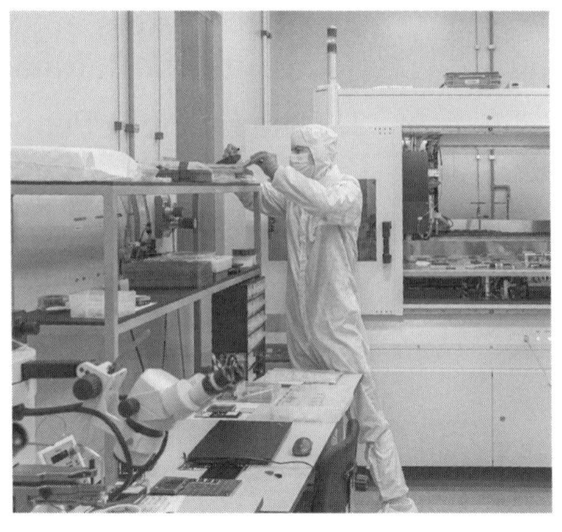

台湾がリトアニアに「代表部」を設置したことで、
中国の怒りの矛先がリトアニア製品排除に向かい、
半導体メーカーのブロリス社はどうなる？

The New York Times ／ Redux ／アフロ

## *Before you read*

### Republic of Lithuania　リトアニア共和国

面積　65,000km²（九州の1.8倍）
人口　2,790,000人／**首都**　ヴィリニュス
民族　リトアニア人　83.1%／ポーランド人　6％
　　　ロシア人　4.8%／ベラルーシ人　1.1%／ウクライナ人　0.6%
宗教　キリスト教・カトリック
通貨　ユーロ／**政体**　共和制
GDP　558億米ドル／１人当たりのGDP　19,964米ドル

### Republic of Nicaragua　ニカラグア共和国

面積　130,370km²（北海道と九州を合わせた広さ）
人口　6,620,000人／**首都**　マナグア
公用語　スペイン語／**識字率**　67.5%
民族　混血　70%／ヨーロッパ系　17%
　　　アフリカ系　９%／先住民　４%
宗教　キリスト教　82%（カトリック　58.5%／
　　　プロテスタント　23.2%）
通貨　コルドバ・オロ／**政体**　立憲共和制
GDP　126億2,000万米ドル／１人当たりGDP　1,943米ドル

### Taiwan　台湾

面積　36,000km²（九州より少し小さい）
人口　23,400,000人／**主要都市**　台北、台中、高雄
言語　中国語、台湾語、客家語／**識字率**　98.3%
民族　台湾原住の本省人　85%／中国本土からの外省人　15%
宗教　道教　４%／仏教　0.6%
　　　キリスト教　1.1%（カトリック　0.9%／
　　　プロテスタント　0.2%）
通貨　新台湾ドル／**政体**　民主共和制
GDP　7,727億米ドル／１人当たりのGDP　33,004米ドル

## Words and Phrases

次の１～５の語句の説明として最も近いものをａ～ｅから１つ選び、（　）内に記入しなさい。

| | | | |
|---|---|---|---|
| **1.** cozy up to | (　　) | **a.** anger |
| **2.** lopsided | (　　) | **b.** be friendly with |
| **3.** fend for | (　　) | **c.** uneven or unfair |
| **4.** virtual | (　　) | **d.** look after or take care of |
| **5.** wrath | (　　) | **e.** online |

## Summary

次の英文は記事の要約です。下の語群から最も適切な語を１つ選び、（　）内に記入しなさい。

2-07

Mainland China fiercely opposes governments that appear to (　　　) Taiwan as independent. After a Taiwanese trade office opened in Vilnius, Beijing (　　　) blocked any product connected, directly or indirectly, with Lithuania. (　　　) 22 among the world's economies, Taiwan strives to be (　　　). But Nicaragua's decision to cut diplomatic relations shows how difficult it is to (　　　) Chinese pressure.

ranked　　recognized　　regard　　resist　　ruthlessly

1990年３月11日、リトアニアは、独立回復を宣言。これはソビエト連邦構成共和国の中で最も早いものであった。国内に他民族（主にロシア人）が少なかったことが、国内意見の集約を容易にさせた側面があるとされる。1991年９月６日、ソ連もリトアニアの独立を承認した。また９月17日にはエストニア、ラトビアとともに国際連合に加盟した。なお、独立回復後は、エストニアやラトビアとは異なり、残留ロシア人に対しほぼ無条件でリトアニア国籍を与えている。計画経済から自由経済へ移行したあと、2004年３月29日にNATOへ加盟。さらに５月１日には欧州連合（EU）への加盟を果たした。リトアニアは中華人民共和国を承認しているが、中国の人権問題から不信感を募らせており、2010年代後半より台湾との関係を重視するようになった。2021年11月、台湾外交部はヴィリニュスに駐リトアニア台湾代表処が開設されたが、中華人民共和国は猛反発し、在リトアニア大使館の「臨時代理大使事務所」への格下げに続いて、北京駐在のリトアニア外交官とその家族からの事実上の外交特権剥奪、リトアニア産品やリトアニアの部品を使った工業製品の通関妨害など「報復」を行なっている。

ニカラグアは中央アメリカで最も面積が広い国である。反米左翼ゲリラであるサンディニスタ民族解放戦線（FSLN）の指導者オルテガは、1936年から43年間続いた親米ソモサ一家の独裁政権を打倒した。オルテガは、1984年大統領に初当選したが、1990年の選挙で敗北し、2006年11月に大統領へ再選され、独裁化して行った。強権的な独裁政治が「社会主義者が億万長者になった」と批判される。2021年の大統領選で４期連続５回目の大統領に就任した。オルテガ政権は中華人民共和国、ロシア、ベネズエラ、キューバ、イランとの関係を重視し、アメリカ・EU諸国を厳く批判している。ニカラグアはパレスチナを承認しており、1985年に一時は国交を樹立した中華人民共和国と1990年に断交してから台湾を承認していたが、2021年に台湾と断交して再び中華人民共和国と国交を樹立した。

## Reading

2-08

# In an Uneven Fight With China, a Tiny Country's Brand Becomes Toxic

Toxic：（有害として）排斥される

VILNIUS, Lithuania — A family-owned semiconductor company in Lithuania sold nothing to China, so it did not worry much last year when Beijing, furious at the Baltic nation for cozying up to Taiwan, began blocking imports of milk products, peat and anything else it could find with a "Made in Lithuania" label.

Closing the door on Lithuanian exports, however, was just the start.

2-09

Today, said Kristijonas Vizbaras, a founder of the successful chip maker Brolis Group, anything with a "Lithuanian smell," no matter how faint — say, a German car with a small Lithuanian-made component — risks getting blocked by China.

The lopsided fight between Lithuania, with a population of under three million, and China started last summer over a representative office that Taiwan, a thriving democracy that Beijing claims as Chinese territory, was opening in Vilnius, the Lithuanian capital.

Beijing has taken aim at foreign economies before. In 2010, it halted salmon imports from Norway after the Oslo-based Nobel Peace Prize committee honored a Chinese dissident writer. And in 2020, it blocked agricultural products from Australia after it called for an investigation into the origins of the coronavirus, which was first detected in China.

2-10

The European Union in January filed a complaint against China with the World Trade Organization, calling its actions against Lithuania "illegal and discriminatory," but has otherwise largely left one of its smallest and weakest members to fend for itself. While publicly pledging solidarity with Lithuania, Josep Borrell, the bloc's foreign policy chief, has privately urged it to appease Beijing by having the office represent "Taipei" instead of Taiwan.

VILNIUS：ビリニュス《バルト３国の一つリトアニアの首都》
cozying up to ～：～と親しくなろうとする
peat：ピート、泥炭
chip maker：半導体メーカー
say,：例えば
representative office：代表事務所
democracy：民主主義国
taken aim at ～：～を狙い撃ちにしてきた
dissident：反体制派の
European Union：欧州連合
filed ～ with …：～を…に申し立てた
World Trade Organization：世界貿易機関
discriminatory：差別的な
otherwise：それ以外の点では
fend for itself：自力で何とかする
pledging ～：～を誓約する
solidarity with ～：～との連帯
appease ～：～をなだめる
having：《使役動詞》

Gabrielius Landsbergis, Lithuania's foreign minister and the driving force behind its closer ties with Taiwan, traveled to France in January for a meeting of E.U. foreign ministers, but secured little support beyond vague promises of solidarity.

beyond ～：～を凌駕する、～以上の

By Andrew Higgins
*The New York Times, February 21, 2022*

2-11

## Taiwan Loses Nicaragua as Ally as Tensions With China Rise

Nicaragua：ニカラグア《中米で最大の国》

as Ally：同盟国としての

Tensions With China：台湾と中国との緊張

Nicaragua has broken diplomatic relations with Taiwan in favor of China, further reducing the number of countries that still recognize the self-governing island as a sovereign nation.

The decision, announced in a statement by Nicaragua's foreign minister on Thursday local time, dealt a blow to the progress Taiwan had recently made to win broader international support, if not official recognition.

sovereign nation：主権国家

statement：声明

dealt a blow to ～：～に打撃を与えた

if not official recognition：公式の承認ではないにしても

President Biden invited two Taiwanese officials to join the virtual "summit for democracy" now underway in Washington. The small Baltic nation of Lithuania has provoked China's wrath by agreeing, among other things, to open a trade office with Taiwan under its own name.

"summit for democracy"：「民主主義サミット」

among other things：取り分け

under its own name：実名で、「台湾」という名前で

2-12

Other nations in Eastern Europe, once under the domination of the Soviet Union, have also deepened economic and cultural ties, including the Czech Republic, Poland and Slovakia.

Such efforts have increasingly turned Taiwan into a potential flash point in China's relations with the world, particularly the United States, which has sought to shore up Taiwan's status as a de facto nation with more than 23 million people and the world's 22nd-largest economy by gross domestic product.

flash point：引火点、火種

de facto：事実上の

gross domestic production：国内総生産

By Steven Lee Myers
*The New York Times, December 10, 2021*

## *Exercises*

**Multiple Choice**

次の１～５の英文を完成させるために、a～dの中から最も適切なものを１つ選びなさい。

**1.** China became angry with Lithuania because

- **a.** it had been friendly with Taiwan.
- **b.** it was importing milk products from Taiwan.
- **c.** it blocked the export of dairy products and peat to China.
- **d.** its products had a bad smell.

**2.** In 2010, China stopped importing salmon from Norway because

- **a.** a Chinese scientist received the Nobel Prize in Physics.
- **b.** the Nobel Peace Prize was given to a Chinese writer.
- **c.** the Nobel Prize in Economics was awarded to a Taiwanese economist.
- **d.** a Taiwanese official was honored by the Nobel Prize committee.

**3.** Josep Borrell wanted Lithuania to calm the Chinese by

- **a.** relocating its trade office from Taiwan to China.
- **b.** closing its trade office in Taipei.
- **c.** saying its trade office represented Taipei rather than Taiwan.
- **d.** ceasing its trade with Taiwan.

**4.** Nicaragua broke diplomatic relations with Taiwan

- **a.** in order to please the government in Taipei.
- **b.** and established them with China.
- **c.** because of pressure from the EU.
- **d.** after joining Biden's virtual "summit for democracy."

**5.** Poland and Slovakia also risked making stronger economic and cultural ties with

- **a.** China.
- **b.** Nicaragua.
- **c.** The United States.
- **d.** Taiwan.

## True or False

本文の内容に合致するものにT（True)、合致しないものにF（False）をつけなさい。

(　　) **1.** Taiwan has officially been recognized as a nation by the U.S.A.

(　　) **2.** Taiwan's GDP was the world's twentieth-largest economy in 2021.

(　　) **3.** The E.U. refused to back Lithuania in its dispute with China.

(　　) **4.** In 2020, China blocked dairy products from Australia.

(　　) **5.** German exports could be blocked too if they include Lithuanian components.

## Vocabulary

次の英文は、読売新聞の The Japan News「えいご工房」に掲載された *Biden calls out China's Taiwan actions as 'coercive' at summit*『バイデン大統領　首脳会議で中国の台湾に対する行動を「威圧的」と指摘』の記事の一部です。下の語群から最も適切なものを１つ選び、（　）内に記入しなさい。

Kuala Lumpur (AP) — U.S. President Joe Biden told leaders at the East Asia Summit on Wednesday that China's recent actions in the Taiwan Strait are "coercive" and undermined peace and (　　　) in the region.

The comments by Biden, who participated by video in the annual meeting of 18 Asia-Pacific nations, come during a surge in Chinese (　　　) activity near the island that China regards as a (　　　) province and has vowed to reclaim by force if necessary.

Last week, Biden set off (　　　) bells in Beijing by saying the U.S. has a firm commitment to (　　　) Taiwan defend itself in the event of a Chinese attack.

The White House later (　　　) the president's comments and said he did not mean to imply any changes in the U.S. "one-China policy."

Relations between Washington and Beijing have (　　　) to new lows since (　　　) under former President Donald Trump's administration.

| alarm | downplayed | help | military |
|---|---|---|---|
| nosediving | plunged | renegade | stability |

Unit 16

# ●スリランカ　有機農法を始めて大惨事に

経済危機に陥ったスリランカのコロンボで野菜を買い求める人々　AFP／WAA

## *Before you read*

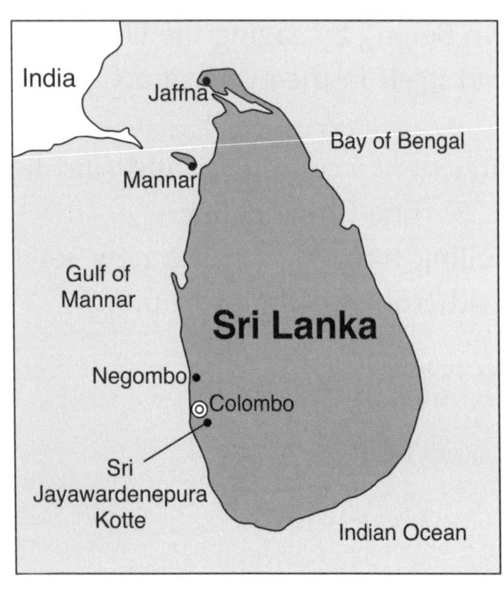


Democratic Socialist Republic of Sri Lanka
スリランカ民主社会主義共和国

面積　65,610km²（北海道の約0.8倍）
首都　スリ・ジャヤワルダナプラ・コッテ
公用語　シンハラ語・タミル語
人口　21,920,000人
民族　シンハラ人　74.9%／タミル人　15.3%
　　　スリランカ・ムーア人　9.3%
宗教　仏教　70.1%／ヒンドゥ教　12.6%
　　　イスラム教　9.7%／キリスト教　7.6%
識字率　92.5%
GDP　807億米ドル
　　　1人当たりGDP　3,682米ドル
通貨　ルピー
政体　共和制

## Words and Phrases

次の１～５の語の説明として最も近いものをａ～ｅから１つ選び、（　）内に記入しなさい。

**1.** pesticide　(　　)
**2.** reap　(　　)
**3.** spiral　(　　)
**4.** reversal　(　　)
**5.** unsnarl　(　　)

**a.** harvest or gather
**b.** soar
**c.** chemical used to destroy bugs
**d.** unblock
**e.** adoption of an earlier policy

## Summary

次の英文は記事の要約です。下の語群から最も適切な語を１つ選び、（　）内に記入しなさい。

2-13

Sri Lanka's government said it stopped importing chemical fertilizers to make food (　　　). Some people, however, think the main (　　　) was to save money. Lockdowns and the (　　　) of tourism hit the local economy badly and limited funds for imports. Unfortunately, organic farming seems to have reduced agricultural (　　　). Food prices have (　　　), and the government has had to reverse its decision.

safer　　soared　　reason　　suspension　　yields

スリランカ共和国は、インド洋の真珠とも言われる緑豊かな熱帯の島で、面積は北海道の約８割。紅茶の生産が盛んで、主要産業は農業と繊維業。人口は約2,167万人、最大都市はコロンボ、首都はスリ・ジャヤワルダナプラ・コッテである。1948年にイギリスから自治領セイロンとして独立。1972年にはスリランカ共和国に改称し、英連邦内の共和国となった。公用語はシンハラ語とタミル語で、国民の¾がシンハラ人で構成され、国民の７割が仏教徒（上座部仏教）である。

スリランカは経常赤字の拡大と輸入インフレの加速が進み、深刻な経済危機に直面している。外貨不足により資源や食糧などの輸入が困難になったことが背景にある。以前から多額の債務を抱えている点で経済構造が脆弱であり、いつ危機に直面してもおかしくないと指摘されてきた。スリランカは2000年代以降、自国での資金調達が難しいことから対外借入を拡大することでインフラ投資を実施し、高成長を目指した。しかし、2017年には融資の返済に行き詰まったことから、中国企業にハンバントタ港の運営権を99年間、引き渡さざるを得なくなるなど、いわゆる「債務のわな」に陥った。さらに、新型コロナ感染拡大によって観光業が低迷し、外貨の獲得が困難となった。ウクライナ問題に端を発する輸入価格上昇が加わり、化学肥料輸入禁止し、有機農業を推進したが、経済危機を免れることができない。2022年７月14日大統領はシンガポールへ逃亡し、辞表を出した。

## Reading

2-14

# Sri Lanka's Plunge Into Organic Farming Brings Disaster

RATNAPURA, Sri Lanka — This year's crop worries M.D. Somadasa. For four decades, he has sold carrots, beans and tomatoes grown by local farmers using foreign-made chemical fertilizers and pesticides, which helped them reap bigger and richer crops from the verdant hills that ring his hometown.

Then came Sri Lanka's sudden, and disastrous, turn toward organic farming. The government campaign, ostensibly driven by health concerns, lasted only seven months. But farmers and agriculture experts blame the policy for a sharp drop in crop yields and spiraling prices that are worsening the country's growing economic woes and leading to fears of food shortages.

2-15

Prices for some foodstuffs, like rice, have risen by nearly one-third compared with a year ago, according to Sri Lanka's central bank. The prices of vegetables like tomatoes and carrots have risen to five times their year-ago levels.

Late last month, Sri Lanka's plantation minister, Ramesh Pathirana, confirmed a partial reversal of the policy, telling the country's Parliament that the government would be importing fertilizer necessary for tea, rubber and coconut, which make up the nation's major agricultural exports.

"We will be importing fertilizers depending on the requirement in the country," Mr. Pathirana told The New York Times. "So far, we don't have enough chemical fertilizers in the country because we didn't import them."

2-16

Food costs are rising around the world as pandemic-related supply chain knots are slowly unsnarled and as prices rise for feedstocks like natural gas that are used to make fertilizer and other supplies. Sri Lanka added to those pressures with its own missteps.

Sri Lanka：スリランカ《インド南のインド洋にあるセイロン島の国》

Plunge Into ～：急に～し始めること

Organic Farming：有機農法

Disaster：大惨事

crop：収穫高

fertilizers：肥料

pesticides：殺虫剤

prices：物価

leading to ～：～を引き起こす

by：《程度を表す》

reversal：失敗、撤回

make up ～：～を構成する

requirement：要求

Food costs：食品価格

feedstocks：原材料

supplies：生活必需品

added to ～ with …：…で～を増大させた

Chemical fertilizers are essential tools for modern agriculture. Still, governments and environmental groups have grown increasingly concerned about their overuse. They have been blamed for growing water pollution problems, while scientists have found increased risks of colon, kidney and stomach cancer from excessive nitrate exposure.

2-17

President Gotabaya Rajapaksa cited health concerns when his government banned the importation of chemical fertilizers in April, a pledge he had initially made during his 2019 election campaign.

"Sustainable food systems are part of Sri Lanka's rich sociocultural and economic heritage," he told a United Nations summit in September.

Mr. Rajapaksa's critics pointed to another reason: Sri Lanka's dwindling reserves of money.

2-18

Covid-19 lockdowns devastated Sri Lanka's tourist industry, which generates one-tenth of the country's economic output and provides a major source of foreign currency. The domestic currency, the rupee, has lost about one-fifth of its value, limiting Sri Lanka's ability to purchase food and supplies abroad just as prices were rising. That added to lingering problems like its huge debt load, including on high-interest loans from Chinese state banks that required it to take out still more loans.

"Our annual earnings from tourism amounting to almost $5 billion did not materialize during the last two years," Basil Rajapaksa, the finance minister and the president's brother, told Parliament last month. "As a government, we acknowledge that our foreign reserves are being challenged."

As Sri Lanka's economy struggled and global prices rose, its foreign exchange reserves shrank by about 70 percent. Shaving foreign-made fertilizer from the country's shopping list would help stem the slide.

By Aanya Wipulasena and Mujib Mashal
*The New York Times, December 7, 2021*

water pollution：水質汚染

nitrate exposure：硝酸塩露出

reserves of money：準備金

Covid-19：新型コロナウイルス感染症による

economic output：経済産出量

debt load：借金

including on ～：～に書き入れる

take out loans：融資を受ける

materialize：具現化する、実現する

foreign reserves：外貨準備高

challenged：欠けている、足りない

foreign exchange reserves：外貨準備高、外国為替予備金

stem the slide：滑落を食い止める

## *Exercises*

### Multiple Choice

次の１～５の英文を完成させるために、a～dの中から最も適切なものを１つ選びなさい。

**1.** In April 2019, Sri Lanka banned the import of chemical fertilizers

**a.** to raise crop yields.
**b.** because pesticides destroy bugs.
**c.** to make food safer.
**d.** because of soaring food prices.

**2.** Since the move to organic farming, carrots

**a.** have become five times costlier.
**b.** are up to one-third pricier.
**c.** are even more expensive than tomatoes.
**d.** can no longer be imported.

**3.** ________________ hit Sri Lankan tourism badly.

**a.** Drops in crop yields
**b.** Soaring prices
**c.** The falling rupee
**d.** Covid lockdowns

**4.** Some critics say the government was more interested in ______________ than promoting healthy farming.

**a.** saving money
**b.** promoting tourism
**c.** raising crop yields
**d.** borrowing money from China

**5.** The Sri Lankan currency, the rupee,

**a.** has fallen by around 50%.
**b.** has lost nearly one-fourth of its value.
**c.** has gone down by about 20%.
**d.** has weakened five times.

## True or False

本文の内容に合致するものにＴ（True）、合致しないものにＦ（False）をつけなさい。

(　　) **1.** The Sri Lankan government suddenly stopped exporting chemical fertilizers to save money.

(　　) **2.** President Gotabaya Rajapaksa discussed health issues during his election campaign.

(　　) **3.** There is no risk of colon cancer from chemical fertilizers.

(　　) **4.** The economic crisis made the government completely reverse its policy on fertilizers.

(　　) **5.** The government has been heavily in debt recently.

## Vocabulary

次の１～８は「農業」に関する語句です。該当する英語説明文を下のａ～ｈの中から１つ選び、(　)に入れなさい。

**1.** agriculture (　　)
**2.** chemical fertilizer (　　)
**3.** crop-dusting (　　)
**4.** dairy farming (　　)
**5.** horticulture (　　)
**6.** nursery (　　)
**7.** organic farming (　　)
**8.** pesticide (　　)

**a.** a chemical substance added to soil to make it more fertile
**b.** a chemical substance used to kill small animals or insects harming food supplies
**c.** sprinkling insecticide on crops from the air
**d.** growing crops or raising animals for food
**e.** the practice or science of growing fruit, flowers and vegetables
**f.** a method of farming in which food is grown without the help of artificial substances
**g.** the business of producing, storing and distributing milk and its products
**h.** a place where plants and trees are reared for sale or transplantation

Unit **17**

# ●トンガ　自然の猛威被害が３度目

南太平洋、トンガ沖の海底火山の噴火で新たな島が出現　AFP／WAA

## *Before you read*

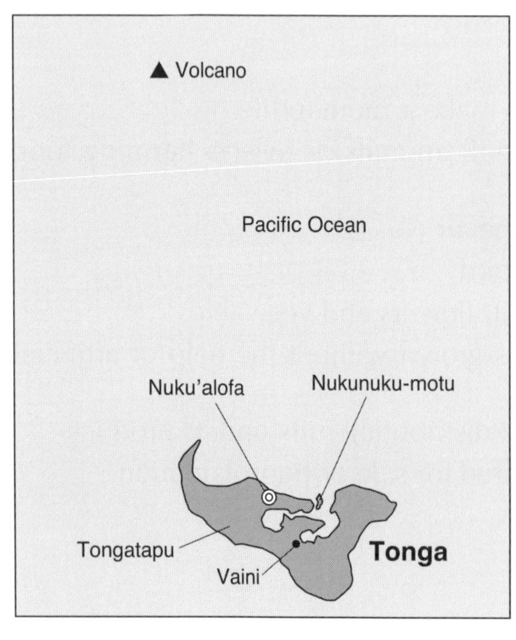


Kingdom of Tonga
トンガ王国

面積　720km²（対馬とほぼ同じ）
人口　105,697人
首都　ヌクアロファ
公用語　トンガ語、英語
民族　ポリネシア人　98%
宗教　キリスト教（プロテスタント、モルモン教）　99%
GDP　４億9,000万米ドル
　１人当たりGDP　4,979米ドル
通貨　パアンガ
識字率　99.4%
政体　立憲君主制

## Words and Phrases

次の１～５の語句の説明として最も近いものをａ～ｅから１つ選び、（　）内に記入しなさい。

**1.** wipe out　（　　）
**2.** withstand　（　　）
**3.** trigger　（　　）
**4.** in disguise　（　　）
**5.** quitter　（　　）

**a.** cause
**b.** hidden or unexpected
**c.** someone who gives up
**d.** resist
**e.** destroy

## Summary

次の英文は記事の要約です。下の語群から最も適切な語を１つ選び、（　）内に記入しなさい。

2-19

Ha'atafu beach resort in Tonga has been (　　　) three times. The family that owns it (　　　) everything after cyclones in 1982 and 1993. They survived another cyclone in 2020 with little (　　　). But then came a volcanic (　　　) and tsunami in 2022. Although rebuilding was delayed by the island nation's first Covid-linked (　　　), they are determined to continue.

damage　destroyed　eruption　lockdown　rebuilt

トンガ王国は171の島からなる群島であり、そのうち45が居住地である。2021年現在、トンガの人口は105,697人で、その70%が本島のトンガタプ島に居住している。国土は南北に約800km 広がっている。約2,500年前にラピタ族が最初に居住し、ポリネシア系住民が徐々にトンガ人としての明確な民族的アイデンティティ、言語、文化を発展させ、いち早く南太平洋に強力な足場を築き、地域の大国へと成長した。

1900年から1970年まで、トンガはイギリスの保護国であった。イギリスは友好条約に基づき、トンガの外交を担当したがトンガはいかなる外国勢力にも主権を放棄しなかった。立法改革が最初の部分的代表選挙への道を開いた後の2010年、トンガは伝統的な絶対王政から脱却し完全な立憲君主制へと移行するため一歩を踏み出した。

2022年１月15日13時頃トンガで海底火山の大規模な噴火があった。当初遠く離れた日本への影響はあまりないと予測されていたが、夜になって、日本の各地に津波が押し寄せた。気圧の変化で海面が変動し、津波を引き起こしたのではないかと専門家は指摘している。津波の前には必ず強い揺れがあるはずだという思い込みは、かえって災害が起きたときの柔軟な対応を阻害しかねない。トンガは浸水や通信の寸断で状況の把握が進んでいない。私の30年来の友人で、トンガの文部大臣に就任したことのあるマサソ氏に e-mail を入れ、安否を気遣ったら、15分後くらいに大丈夫だと知らせがあった。2014年３月にトンガを訪問した際、国王トゥポウ６世に謁見することができた。津波警報器は日本から贈られたと喜んでおられた。

## Reading

2-20

# 'We just keep going': the Tongan resort destroyed by nature's fury — for the third time

Despite a narrow escape from last month's tsunami and the arrival of Covid in Tonga, Ha'atafu manager Moana Paea is determined to rebuild her resort once again.

When the Ha'atafu beach resort was levelled by the tsunami that hit Tonga last month, it was the third time that the family-run business had been completely destroyed by a natural disaster.

In 1982, the resort was wiped out by Cyclone Isaac and 11 years later by Cyclone Kina.

2-21

Back then, the resort was run by Australian Steve Burling and his Tongan wife, Sesika. Now their daughter Moana Paea, and her husband, Hola, have taken over its running.

"My only memory of Kina is arriving back to Tonga to no home. My dad started building the place while living in a tent," said Paea.

After the second wipeout, Paea's father rebuilt the resort inland with more cyclone-resilience measures, including trees being planted all over the property.

2-22

"This [has] proven a great strategy for us as we withstood some great big cyclones over those 28 years, especially Cyclone Harold which wiped out the west coast two years ago. We only had minor damages then."

But the resort has never had to stand up to a tsunami before.

When the Hunga Tonga-Hunga Ha'apai volcano erupted on 15 January, triggering a tsunami, Paea's business was one of seven resorts to be wiped out on the western side of Tongatapu, the Pacific nation's main island.

"With a tsunami, it just comes and it takes everything. You're never prepared," says Paea.

2-23

The disaster killed four people and caused US$90.4m (TOP 208M) in damages to Tonga, according to the World Bank,

Tongan：トンガの《ポリネシアに位置する立憲君主制国家》

resort：リゾート施設

fury：猛威

narrow escape：間一髪の命拾い

Ha'atafu：ハアタフ《リゾート施設名》

levelled：跡形もなくなった

wiped out：徹底的に破壊された

Cyclone：サイクロン、低気圧《インド洋・南太平洋ではサイクロン、北太平洋ではタイフーン、北大西洋はハリケーン》

Isaac：アイザック《サイクロンは ABC 順で人名を付ける》

Back then：当時

to no home：家が全く無くなった《結果を表す》

place：自宅

inland：海から離れた所に《副詞》

resilience：耐性

property：地所

withstood ～：～に持ちこたえた

stand up to ～：～に耐える、立ち向かう

business：会社、事業所

(TOP 208M)：フランスの自動車メーカー、プジョーの最高級車種208M も含まれる

World Bank：世界銀行《国際開発金融機関》

equivalent to 18.5% of Tonga's GDP. Residents of three of the worst affected islands who lost their homes have been relocated to the main island of Tongatapu. The fibre optic cable connecting Tonga to the world was broken and was only repaired this week, leaving Tonga with an internet blackout for more than a month.

Rebuilding in Tonga has been complicated by the fact that a week after the tsunami Tonga, which had until that point recorded only a single case of Covid during the entire pandemic, was hit by an outbreak of the virus. Strict lockdowns were imposed, and Tonga seems to have contained it, with just under 300 cases reported.

2-24

But for the Paea family, who have been staying with a friend since the tsunami destroyed their home, lockdown has been a blessing in disguise.

“It has made us stop and rest. Otherwise we would [have] carried on with planting trees and moving forward.

“After the tsunami we didn't cry much with losing everything ... Our kids, especially our 11-year-old, had cried missing our home. So the lockdown had given us time to grieve.”

Now that the lockdown has eased, the family will start rebuilding.

“We're not quitters. Just because we go through some hardship doesn't mean we quit. We just keep going.”

By Taina Kami Enoka

*The Guardian , February 25, 2022*

equivalent to ～：～に相当する

fibre optic cable：光ファイバー・ケーブル

blackout：喪失、使用不能

outbreak：（感染の）大流行

contained ～：～を封じ込めた

blessing in disguise：不幸中の幸い、災難に見えるが実は有難いこと

carried on with ～：～を続行した

cry with ～：～したことで泣く

quitters：簡単に諦める人

Just because ～：～だからといって《主語となっている：it を補うと分かり易い》

hardship：苦労、辛いこと

## *Exercises*

### Multiple Choice

次の１の英文の質問に答え、２～５の英文を完成させるために、a～dの中から最も適切なものを１つ選びなさい。

**1.** How does the Paea family's latest disaster differ from their previous misfortunes?

**a.** They had to pause before getting on with recovery because of a lockdown.
**b.** They gave up after enduring just too many crises.
**c.** Their resort was completely destroyed.
**d.** They were prepared for a tsunami and did not suffer much damage.

**2.** In 1993, Ha'atafu beach resort was destroyed by

**a.** Cyclone Isaac.
**b.** Cyclone Kina.
**c.** Cyclone Harold.
**d.** Covid-19.

**3.** In 2020, Paea's beach resort

**a.** suffered severe loss.
**b.** suffered little damage.
**c.** totally collapsed.
**d.** survived with no damage.

**4.** In 2022, Ha'atafu was wiped out by

**a.** a tsunami following the eruption of an undersea volcano.
**b.** an earthquake triggered by a volcanic eruption.
**c.** flooding and heavy winds caused by a cyclone.
**d.** a one-month blackout throughout Tongatapu.

**5.** From this latest disaster, Tonga's loss was equivalent to

**a.** 19.5% of its GDI.
**b.** 17.5% of its GDI.
**c.** 18.5% of its GDP.
**d.** 16.5% of its GDP.

## True or False

本文の内容に合致するものにT（True）、合致しないものにF（False）をつけなさい。

(　　) **1.** The Paea family's business has been destroyed four times.

(　　) **2.** Before the undersea volcano erupted, Tonga had not recorded a single case of Covid.

(　　) **3.** After imposing lockdowns, Tonga had over 300 cases of Covid.

(　　) **4.** Although their home was wiped out, lockdown for the Paea family helped them recover mentally.

(　　) **5.** In addition to Ha'atafu, seven other resorts were wiped out in 2022.

## Vocabulary

次の英文は、読売新聞のThe Japan News「えいご工房」に掲載された*Fishermen protest eruption-induced oil spill in Peru*『噴火によるペルーの原油流出に漁師ら反発』の記事の一部です。下の語群から最も適切なものを1つ選び、（　）内に記入しなさい。

LIMA (AP) — An oil (　　　) on the Peruvian coast caused by the waves from an (　　　) of an undersea volcano in the South Pacific nation of Tonga prompted dozens of (　　　) to protest Jan. 18, outside the South American country's main oil refinery.

The men gathered outside the (　　　) in the province of Callao near Lima. Peru's environment minister, Ruben Ramirez, told reporters that authorities estimate 6,000 barrels of oil were spilled in an area rich in marine (　　　).

Under the eyes of police, the fishermen carried a large Peruvian flag, fishing nets and signs that read "no to (　　　) crime," "economically affected families" and "Repsol killer of (　　　) fauna," which refers to the Spain-based company that manages the La Pampilla refinery, which processes about 117,000 barrels of oil a day, according to its website.

Fifty workers from companies that work for Repsol inside the refinery removed the (　　　) sand with shovels and piled it up on a small promontory.

| | | | |
|---|---|---|---|
| biodiversity | ecological | eruption | fishermen |
| marine | oil-stained | refinery | spill |

Unit **18**

# ●ベンガル湾で大洪水　住民はマングローブの森に避難

インド、増水被害軽減に向け、マングローブの植林に従事する女性たち
The New York Times ／ Redux ／アフロ

## *Before you read*

**Republic of India　インド共和国**

面積　3,287,590km²（日本の8.7倍）（世界７位）
人口　1,310,000,000人（世界２位）
首都　ニューデリー／デリー連邦直轄地
最大都市　ムンバイ
公用語　英語、ヒンドゥ語／識字率　75.6%
民族　インド・アーリア族　72%
　　　ドラヴィダ族　25%／モンゴロイド族　３%
宗教　ヒンドゥ教　79.8%／イスラム教　14.2%
　　　キリスト教　2.3%／シーク教　1.7%
　　　仏教　0.7%／ジャイナ教　0.4%
GDP　２兆7,187億米ドル（世界７位）
　　　１人当たり GDP　2,038米ドル（世界144位）
通貨　インド・ルピー
政体　共和制

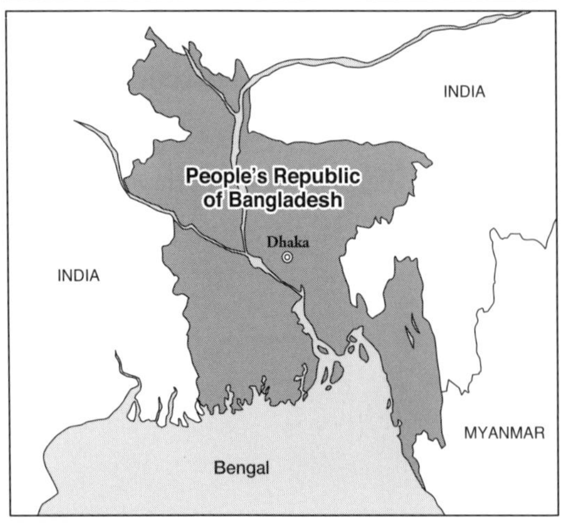


**People's Republic of Bangladesh**
**バングラディシュ人民共和国**

面積　215,000km²（日本の約40%）
人口　164,680,000人
公用語　ベンガル語／識字率　72.9%
首都　ダッカ
民族　ベンガル人が大部分
宗教　イスラム教　90.4%
　　　ヒンドゥ教・仏教・キリスト教　9.6%
GDP　2,149億米ドル
　　　１人当たり GDP　1,968米ドル
通貨　タカ
政体　共和制

## Words and Phrases

次の１～５の語句の説明として最も近いものをａ～ｅから１つ選び、(　) 内に記入しなさい。

| | | | |
|---|---|---|---|
| **1.** straddle | (　　) | **a.** | spread across two sides/countries |
| **2.** bolster | (　　) | **b.** | in imminent danger of |
| **3.** salinity | (　　) | **c.** | reinforce |
| **4.** nurture | (　　) | **d.** | help something small grow bigger |
| **5.** on the edge of | (　　) | **e.** | saltiness |

## Summary

次の英文は記事の要約です。下の語群から最も適切な語を１つ選び、(　) 内に記入しなさい。

2-25

In tropical coastal areas, mangrove forests lower the (　　　) of flooding by weakening waves. They also (　　　) greenhouse gases. So, after a powerful cyclone hit the Sundarbans, local inhabitants (　　　) the advice of conservationists and started planting mangrove (　　　). Most of the activists are women, and as well as (　　　) their villages they have found ways to increase their incomes.

followed　　protecting　　reduce　　risk　　saplings

スンダルバンス国立公園（Sundarbans National Park）は、インド共和国・西ベンガル州に所在する国立公園。世界最大規模を有するデルタ地帯の一画を占め、数多くの希少種や絶滅危惧種が生息している。この国立公園は、バングラデシュとの国境に近いインド東部の西ベンガル州南端に所在し、ベンガル湾の奥にひろがる東西およそ250km、南北40～80km におよぶ、世界最大のデルタ（三角州）地帯のなかに立地する。ヒマラヤ山脈より流下するガンジス川とブラマプトラ川は、数百万年前から山地より大量の土砂を運んで下流に巨大な堆積平野を形成してきた。デルタ地帯は表面積80,000km² に及び、川は天然の水路となって網目状に入り組んでいる。

デルタを形成する水路の沿岸には世界最大規模のマングローブの密林が広がっており、これは当地方に多数発生する暴風雨に対する自然の防波堤の役目を担っている。また、干潮の際にすがたを見せるマングローブの強力な気根は、水中の土砂の流出を食い止めて陸地を形成するのに大きく作用してきた。大河によって運ばれてきた泥はマングローブの根のあいだに厚く堆積してきたのである。なお、スンダルバンス国立公園に近接するバングラデシュ側のシュンドルボンも1997年、世界遺産に登録された。マングローブの密生する湿地帯には300種を超える植物が生育し、数多くの水生・陸生動物のすみかとなっている。また、干潟は上流より運ばれてきた養分豊かな土壌となっているため、数多くの海洋動物はここで孵化期を過ごしている。

## Reading

2-26

# Facing Disastrous Floods, They Turned to Mangrove Trees for Protection

LAKSHMIPUR, India — As sea levels rise, eroding embankments and pushing water closer to their doorsteps, the residents of the hundreds of villages in the Sundarbans — an immense network of rivers, tidal flats, small islands and vast mangrove forests straddling India and Bangladesh — have found their lives and livelihoods at risk.

In the absence of much government support, women like Aparna Dhara, with help from a nonprofit environmental conservation organization, have devised their own solution: planting hundreds of thousands of additional mangrove trees to bolster their role as protective barriers.

2-27

After Cyclone Aila slammed into the region in 2009, causing floods and mudslides, nearly 200 people lost their lives.

Amid the rising waters, crocodiles have begun entering villages. And higher salinity in the water has killed off fish "as if the entire area had been crushed under the thumb," said Ajanta Dey, a Kolkata-based conservationist.

A few years ago, as Ms. Dey went around documenting the post-cyclone wreckage, women like Ms. Dhara approached her and pointed to areas where their homes had once stood. Ms. Dey suggested planting more mangroves between existing embankments and open water. By 2015, over 15,000 women had signed up to for the mission, according to Ms. Dey, program director at Nature Environment and Wildlife Society.

2-28

While all are welcome to participate, many men from the Sundarbans migrate to cities for work, meaning it's the villages' women who are often leading the climate change fight.

The women, drawing on their deep knowledge of

- LAKSHMIPUR：《インドのオリッサ州コラプット地方にある都市》
- eroding ～：～を侵食する
- embankments：堤防
- tidal flat：干潟
- straddling ～ and …：～と…とに跨る
- at risk：危険に曝されている
- nonprofit environmental conservation organization：非営利の環境保護団体
- solution：解決方法
- mudslides：土砂崩れ
- salinity：塩分濃度
- documenting ～：～を記録する
- wreckage：残骸
- open water：開放水域
- signed up to for ～：～に登録した
- Nature Environment and Wildlife Society：自然環境及び野生生物協会
- it's ～ that：《強調構文》
- drawing on ～：～を利用する

the Sundarbans, make hand-drawn maps of areas where mangroves can be planted. They nurture seeds into saplings and then, in baskets or on boats, transport the young trees and dig in the mud flats to plant them. Later, they track their growth on a mobile app.

2-29

In Ms. Dhara's village, Lakshmipur, the number of acres covered with mangroves has grown to 2,224 from 343 in the last decade. In areas that had been barren-looking mud flats just a few years ago, cranes, gulls and herons abound in the flat rounded leaves of the mangrove trees.

Mangroves, found only in tropical and subtropical climates, are distinctive for their ability to survive in brackish water. Research has shown mangrove forests to be an excellent way to mitigate the effects of climate change, especially the storm surge accompanying cyclones, by reducing the height and speed of waves. Mangroves also help reduce greenhouse gases, as they have high rates of carbon capture.

2-30

While many in the village share her sense of living on the edge of a climate disaster, Ms. Dhara said it nonetheless seemed impossible at first to persuade her family to let her join the group of women planting mangroves back in 2013.

But Ms. Dhara persisted, and was able to convince her family that the trees would not only help keep the village safe from floods, but were also a chance to earn extra income. Ms. Dey's organization pays the women for growing and planting mangrove saplings, and also helps them sell fish, vegetables, honey, eggs and other local goods.

By Suhasini Raj

*The New York Times, April 10, 2022*

nurture 〜 into …：〜を育てて…にする
saplings：苗木、若木
acres：エーカー《面積単位で約4,000㎡》
abound in 〜：〜に沢山いる
distinctive for 〜：〜が特徴だ
brackish water：汽水
mitigate 〜：〜を緩和させる
storm surge：高潮
accompanying 〜：〜に伴う
rates of carbon capture：炭素吸収率
on the edge of 〜：〜の危機に瀕して
persuade 〜 to …：…するように〜を説得する
persisted：何度も粘って主張した
convince 〜 that …：…だと〜を納得させる
extra income：副収入

## Exercises

### Multiple Choice

次の１～５の英文を完成させるために、a～dの中から最も適切なものを１つ選びなさい。

**1.** The village women decided to

**a.** plant mangrove trees to attract tourism.
**b.** plant mangrove trees to protect themselves from floods.
**c.** dig embankments to deter crocodiles.
**d.** dig embankments to provide extra income.

**2.** In 2009, Cyclone Aila caused floods, and ____________ began entering villages.

**a.** crocodiles
**b.** dead fish
**c.** gulls
**d.** cranes

**3.** The women in the Sundarbans ____________ mangrove seeds into saplings and then carry the young trees and ____________ them into the mud flats.

**a.** educate ～ plant
**b.** train ～ plant
**c.** nurture ～ dig
**d.** plant ～ nurture

**4.** The article states that mangroves are found in tropical and subtropical climates in

**a.** sweet water.
**b.** clear water.
**c.** salty water.
**d.** running water.

**5.** Mangrove forests can ____________________ and reduce greenhouse gases.

**a.** increase the effects of floods
**b.** decrease the supply of fish
**c.** raise threats from wildlife
**d.** lessen harm from climate warming

## True or False

本文の内容に合致するものにＴ（True）、合致しないものにＦ（False）をつけなさい。

(　　) **1.** Ms. Dhara planted mangrove trees because they would not only protect the village from floods but also bring extra income for women.

(　　) **2.** The Sundarbans women planted pine trees for protection against floods and erosion.

(　　) **3.** Mangroves now cover 2,224 more acres in Lakshmipur than before.

(　　) **4.** The women used their local knowledge to produce maps of where mangroves could be planted.

(　　) **5.** The replanting project emerged from meetings between village women and Ms. Dey.

## Vocabulary

次の１～７は、日本語の「植え付ける」を使った語句です。日本文に合わせて、下の語群から最も適切なものを１つ選び、（　）内に記入しなさい。

**1.** 子供たちに責任感を植え付ける
(　　　　　　) children a sense of responsibility

**2.** 子供たちの心に彼の名前を植え付ける
(　　　　　　) his name in the heart of children

**3.** 子供たちに相互尊重の念を植え付ける
(　　　　　　) mutual respect among children

**4.** 子供たちに一体感を植え付ける
(　　　　　　) a feeling of unity in children

**5.** 子供たちに地球温暖化の恐ろしさを植え付ける
(　　　　　　) fear of global warming in children

**6.** ウイルスを彼のコンピュータに植え付ける
(　　　　　　) a virus on his computer

**7.** 彼の心に疑いの種を植え付ける
(　　　　　　) a seed of doubt in his mind

| build | carve | give | instill |
|---|---|---|---|
| plant | put | sow | |

Unit **19**

# ● トルコで超インフレとの戦い

物価高の中でトルコ中央銀行が利下げを実施し、インフレがさらに進み、パンも値上がりで庶民は大打撃　　AP／アフロ

## *Before you read*

Republic of Turkey
トルコ共和国
1923年10月29日共和制宣言

面積　780,576km²（日本の約２倍）
人口　83,614,362人
首都　アンカラ
最大都市　イスタンブール
公用語　トルコ語
識字率　95.6%
民族　トルコ人、アルメニア人、ユダヤ人、クルド人
宗教　イスラム教・スンニ派　99%
GDP　7,170億米ドル
　１人当たり GDP　8,599米ドル
通貨　トルコ・リラ
政体　共和制

## Words and Phrases

次の１～５の語句の説明として最も近いものをａ～ｅから１つ選び、(　　) 内に記入しなさい。

**1.** wrench out (　　)
**2.** chuckle (　　)
**3.** crush (　　)
**4.** expansionary (　　)
**5.** compound (　　)

**a.** laugh
**b.** make even worse
**c.** cause to collapse
**d.** pull away by force
**e.** ambitious and aimed at growth

## Summary

次の英文は記事の要約です。下の語群から最も適切な語を１つ選び、(　　) 内に記入しなさい。

2-31

Turkey's (　　　) has halved in value. And now its people are (　　　) the highest inflation in twenty years. One baker says his customers are (　　　) about his prices. But he himself has to pay (　　　) as much for flour. While Turkey is not the only country with inflation, government economic policies seem to have made it worse than (　　　).

| complaining | currency | elsewhere | facing | twice |
|---|---|---|---|---|

トルコ共和国は、西アジアに位置するアナトリア半島（小アジア）と東ヨーロッパに位置するバルカン半島東南端の東トラキア地方を領有する共和制国家。首都はアナトリア中央部のアンカラ。アジアとヨーロッパの２つの大陸にまたがる。11世紀にトルコ系のイスラム王朝の支配の下、イスラム教徒のトルコ人が流入するようになり、土着の諸民族と対立・混交しつつ次第に定着していった。オスマン朝は、15世紀にビザンツ帝国を滅ぼしてイスタンブールを都とし、東はアゼルバイジャンから西はモロッコまで、北はウクライナから南はイエメンまで支配する大帝国を打ち立てる。帝国は、第一次世界大戦で敗北し、英仏伊、ギリシャなどの占領下に置かれ、完全に解体された。1924年に西洋化による近代化を目指すイスラム世界初の世俗主義国家トルコ共和国を建国した。第二次世界大戦後は、ソ連の南部に接するため、反共の防波堤として西側世界に迎えられ、1952年には NATO に、また1961年には OECD に加盟した。

イスラムの復活を望む人々の国内の反体制的な勢力を政治から排除しつつ、西洋化に邁進してきたが、EU への加盟にはクルド問題やキプロス問題、ヨーロッパ諸国の反トルコ・イスラム感情などが障害となっている。2018年の GDP は約7,700億ドルで、世界第19位、１人あたりの GDP は9,405ドルである。2022年２月のロシアのウクライナ侵攻に伴うエネルギーや食糧品価格高騰が直撃し、コロナ禍からの景気回復に水を差している。トルコの３月の消費者物価上昇率は、前年の３月比で61.14%だった。しかし、低金利で生産を増やし、経済が成長すれば、物価も安定すると考え、金融緩和を続けて来ているが、インフレは止まらない。

## Reading

2-32

# Turkey's war with inflation: 'Prices change daily and everyone is scared'

From behind the counter in a bakery in Kasımpaşa, a working-class Istanbul neighbourhood, Mustafa Kafadar can see the orange, white and blue banners of Recep Tayyip Erdoğan's Justice and Development party (AKP) as they blow in the spring breeze.

Kafadar has been wrenched out of retirement by Turkey's economic crisis — his pension is no longer enough to cover his basic expenses. Now he works shifts in the bakery, where he describes living from payday to payday while he sweeps crumbs off a tray.

2-33

"Everything's very expensive. After I buy my essentials and pay my bills, there's nothing left," he says.

Asked who is responsible, he chuckles darkly. "You know who makes inflation high," he says cryptically, reluctant to voice his opinion of Erdoğan's economic policies directly.

Turkey is weathering an unprecedented financial crisis. After the lira lost half its value last year alone, the country is now struggling with rocketing inflation, officially 61.14%.

Kafadar arranges rows of delicate breakfast pastries — fluffy round *açma* filled with olives or chocolate, *börek* and glossy *poğaça* buns — as customers arrive. He tells me they sometimes fly into a rage with him about prices. Jars of pink and white sugared almonds and an entire counter of elegant layer cakes, decorated with fruit and chocolate, sit untouched, now a little too pricey for most.

2-34

"Sugar and wheat prices have gone up. A kilogram bag of flour was 110 lira [£6.15] back in January; now it's 220 lira," he says. Pointing at some of the cheapest buns, he adds: "We couldn't make the prices of the *poğaças* any higher, as people can't afford it."

When Turkey's official inflation rate broke 50% in

scared：怯えている

Istanbul：イスタンブールにある《トルコ最大の都市：首都はアンカラ》

neighbourhood：地域、区域《working-class が修飾》

Justice and Development party：公正発展党

wrenched out of retirement：引退から身をもぎ取られた→引退できず働かざるを得ない

pension：年金

expenses：支出

works shifts：シフト勤務で働く

living from payday to payday：給料ギリギリの暮らし

bills：請求書

cryptically：謎めかして

reluctant to 〜：〜するのを躊躇して

weathering 〜：〜を切り抜けようとしている

lira：トルコ・リラ《トルコの貨幣通貨》

delicate：おいしい

pastries：ペストリー《パイやタルトなど》

fly into a rage：烈火のごとく怒りだす

layer cakes：レイヤー・ケーキ《幾つかの層を重ねて作ったケーキ》

broke 〜：〜を突破した

February, it represented both a two-decade high and a huge political problem for the government. The finance minister, Nureddin Nebati, insisted earlier this month that the surge was “temporary”, while Erdoğan recently vowed to protect Turks against inflation.

2-35 “As the Turkish economy is getting ready to become one of the world’s top 10 economies, we have said that we will not waste this opportunity with careless and thoughtless steps,” he said. “We will get out of this situation in a way that will not crush our citizens with inflation.”

Spiralling inflation is tied to the government’s efforts to radically overhaul the Turkish economy, keeping interest rates low in the belief that this will stimulate it and increase production — against the advice of most experts.

2-36 “Yes, everyone is experiencing inflation worldwide, but Turkey is experiencing it at almost four or five times the rate of others,” says Alp Erinç Yeldan, an economist at Istanbul’s Kadir Has University.

“This is after a series of policy mistakes and ambitious expansionary projects, including following an economic policy that evades the rules of gravity.”

The independent economic research group Enag, which monitors Turkey’s inflation rate using the same metrics as the government, calculates real inflation was 142.63% in March.

Turkey’s financial crisis has been further compounded by Russia’s invasion of Ukraine, which has driven up global food prices, particularly for wheat.

By Ruth Mitchelson and Deniz Bariş Narh
*The Guardian News & Media Ltd, April 16, 2022*

“temporary”：「一時的」
ready to ～：今にも～しそうだ
steps：道のり
overhaul ～：～を見直す
interest rates：金利、利率
after ～：～の結果だ
expansionary：拡大経済の、インフレの
evades ～：～から逃れる
gravity：重力
independent：（国や特定組織から）独立した
Enag：エナグ《インフレ研究グループ》
metrics：指標
compounded：悪化させられた
driven up ～：～を押し上げた

# Exercises

## Multiple Choice

次の１～５の英文を完成させるために、a～dの中から最も適切なものを１つ選びなさい。

**1.** Kafadar's pension

**a.** allows him to enjoy retirement.
**b.** is too small for him to live without working.
**c.** just covers his basic expenses.
**d.** enabled him to buy a bakery.

**2.** In 2021, the Turkish lira

**a.** recovered one third of its value.
**b.** lost half its value.
**c.** recovered half its value.
**d.** lost a quarter of its value.

**3.** Turkey's finance minister emphasized that

**a.** inflation was rocketing.
**b.** economic problems would continue into next year.
**c.** deflation was a bigger problem than inflation.
**d.** the economic crisis was temporary.

**4.** The Turkish government believed that ____________ would augment production and help the economy ____________.

**a.** high interest rates ～ grow
**b.** high interest rates ～ advance
**c.** low interest rates ～ go backward
**d.** low interest rates ～ expand

**5.** Turkey's financial problems have been worsened by

**a.** Covid-19.
**b.** Russia's invasion of Ukraine.
**c.** global inflation.
**d.** the fall of Erdoğan's government.

## True or False

本文の内容に合致するものにＴ（True）、合致しないものにＦ（False）をつけなさい。

( ) **1.** War overseas has helped drive up the price of goods that bakeries buy.

( ) **2.** Turkey's government is in no way the cause of inflation there.

( ) **3.** Kafadar openly criticized the Turkish president's economic policies.

( ) **4.** Few customers at Kafadar's store buy jars of sugared almonds because of the price.

( ) **5.** The Kadir Has economist explained how inflation in other countries is just as bad as in Turkey.

## Vocabulary

次の１～８の語句は、経済に関する反意語です。（ ）内に最も適切な下のａ～ｈの語群、また［ ］内に下のＡ～Ｈの日本語句の説明に入れなさい。

**1.** devaluation ［ ］ ↔ （ ）［平価切上げ］
**2.** （ ）market ［強気市場］ ↔ bear market ［ ］
**3.** inflationary spiral ［ ］ ↔ （ ）spiral ［デフレスパイラル］
**4.** yen's （ ）［円安］ ↔ yen's appreciation ［ ］
**5.** credit （ ）［金融引き締め］ ↔ credit relaxation ［ ］
**6.** trade deficit ［ ］ ↔ trade （ ）［貿易収支黒字］
**7.** economic （ ）［不景気］ ↔ economic booming ［ ］
**8.** creditor country ［ ］ ↔ （ ）country ［債務国］

**a.** bull
**b.** depreciation
**c.** debtor
**d.** deflationary
**e.** revaluation
**f.** slumping
**g.** squeeze
**h.** surplus

**A.** インフレスパイラル
**B.** 円高
**C.** 金融緩和
**D.** 好景気
**E.** 債権国
**F.** 平価切下げ
**G.** 貿易収支赤字
**H.** 弱気市場

# Unit 20

# ●空飛ぶバッテリーでジェット燃料不要

米国ベータ・テクノロジーズ社が試験中の電気式垂直離発着機「アリア」
The New York Times ／ Redux ／アフロ

## *Before you read*

### Questions

**1.** What do you think the article will be about?

この記事は何の話題についてだと思いますか？

**2.** Do you think electrical planes can replace jet-fueled planes?

電気飛行機がジェット燃料飛行機に取って代わることができると思いますか？

## Words and Phrases

次の１～５の語句の説明として最も近いものをａ～ｅから１つ選び、(　) 内に記入しなさい。

| | | | | |
|---|---|---|---|---|
| **1.** | bet on | (　　) | **a.** | having sufficient funds |
| **2.** | trail | (　　) | **b.** | creation or invention |
| **3.** | brainchild | (　　) | **c.** | follow |
| **4.** | propulsion | (　　) | **d.** | gamble on or make a commitment to |
| **5.** | well-financed | (　　) | **e.** | powered driving or movement |

## Summary

次の英文は記事の要約です。下の語群から最も適切な語を１つ選び、(　) 内に記入しなさい。

2-37 Engineers have been producing electric plane (　　　) for decades. Their engines are small, do not need jet fuel, and (　　　) no carbon emissions. But the main problem is that their batteries are (　　　). One Slovenian plane, (　　　) yet quiet, cannot stay in the air for more than an hour. Another plane being tested in Vermont looks (　　　), however.

heavy　　powerful　　promising　　prototypes　　release

ハイブリッドカーや電気自動車が一般的な存在になるにつれて、「電気飛行機は、将来実用化されるのか？」と期待を持つ人が多いはずだ。航空機が膨大な二酸化炭素を排出しているが、すでに電気を動力として用いられている小型の飛行機も存在する。実際に電気飛行機による飛行実験も行われ、今後数年以内に小型の電気飛行機が市場に出回る可能性があると認められている。大型航空機の場合、ジェット燃料のエネルギー密度は最新のリチウムイオン・バッテリーの30倍にも達するそうだ。そのため、ジェット燃料をそのまま同じ体積のリチウムイオン・バッテリーに置き換えても、飛行に必要なだけのエネルギーが供給できないという問題が発生している。

大型旅客機における電化が難しい一方で、全体の重量に占める燃料の割合が10～20％程度である５～10人乗りの小型航空機においては、比較的電動が実用化しやすい。既存の燃料をそのままバッテリーに置き換えるとやはり航行距離が短くなってしまうが、たとえば乗客用のスペースを２～３人分減らしてバッテリーにすることで、従来の燃料で1000kmほど飛行する航空機を500～750kmほど飛行させることが可能なようだ。「リチウム空気バッテリー」は空気中の酸素を正極活物質として充放電可能なバッテリーである。

## Reading

2-38

# The Battery That Flies

> A new aircraft being built in Vermont has no need for jet fuel.
> It can take off and land without a runway.
> Amazon and the Air Force are both betting on it.So who will be in the cockpit?

Kitty Hawk. The invention of the jet engine. And on a frozen Vermont morning, circling above Lake Champlain, the Alia.

In the mind of Christopher Caputo, a pilot, each moment signals a paradigm shift in aviation.

2-39

"You're looking at history," Mr. Caputo said recently, speaking from the cockpit of a plane trailing the Alia at close distance.

It is, essentially, a flying battery. And it represented a long-held aviation goal: an aircraft with no need for jet fuel and therefore no carbon emissions, a plane that could take off and land without a runway and quietly hop from recharging station to recharging station, like a large drone.

The Alia was made by Beta Technologies, where Mr. Caputo is a flight instructor. A five-year-old start-up that is unusual in many respects, the company is the brainchild of Martine Rothblatt, the founder of Sirius XM and pharmaceutical company United Therapeutics, and Kyle Clark, a Harvard-trained engineer and former professional hockey player.

2-40

A battery-powered aircraft with no internal combustion has been a goal of engineers ever since the Wright brothers. Larry Page, the Google co-founder, has been funding electric plane start-ups for over a decade. Electric motors have the virtue of being smaller, allowing more of them to be fitted on a plane and making it easier to design systems with vertical lift. However, batteries are heavy, planes need to be light, and for most of the last century, the e-plane was thought to be beyond reach.

- Vermont：バーモント州《米国北東部の州》
- Air Force：空軍
- betting on 〜：〜に賭ける
- Kitty Hawk：キティーホーク《ノースカロライナ州にあるライト兄弟が初飛行に成功した地》
- Alia：アリア《電気垂直航空機の名》
- paradigm shift：パラダイムシフト《支配的な理論の基礎となる前提が劇的に変化することに》
- aviation：航空
- hop from 〜 to …：〜から…へ渡り歩く
- recharging station：充電スタンド
- start-up：新興企業
- brainchild：発案物
- Sirius XM：シリウスXM《衛星ラジオ放送会社》
- pharmaceutical：製薬の
- Harvard-trained：ハーバード大学で教育を受けた
- internal combustion：内燃機関
- Wright brothers：ライト兄弟《動力飛行機の発明者かつ世界初の飛行機パイロット》
- virtue：利点
- vertical lift：垂直上昇

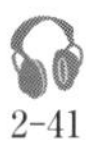
2-41

That changed with the extraordinary gains in aviation technology realized since the 1990s.

Late last year, curious about the potential of so-called green aviation, I flew in a Pipistrel Alpha Electro, a sleek new Slovenian two-seater designed for flight training. The Electro looks and flies like an ordinary light aircraft, but absent the roar of internal combustion, its single propeller makes a sound like beating wings. "Whoa!" I exclaimed when its high-torque engine caused it to practically leap off the runway.

However, the Electro's power supply lasts only about an hour. After ours nearly ran out, I wondered how many people would enjoy flying in an electric plane. That take off is fun. But then you do start to worry about the landing.

2-42

Despite the excitement about e-planes, the Federal Aviation Administration has never certified electric propulsion as safe for commercial use. Companies expect that to change in the coming years, but only gradually, as safety concerns are worked out. As that process occurs, new forms of aviation are likely to appear, planes never seen before outside of testing grounds.

Propelled by advances in batteries, control systems and high performance motors, more than a dozen well-financed competitors have their own prototypes, nearly all focused on what the industry calls "urban air mobility," or flying taxis or privately owned flying vehicles.

By Ben Ryder Howe
*The New York Times, April 16, 2022*

gains：進歩
green：グリーン、環境に優しい
sleek：流線型の格好良い
beating wings：羽をバタバタ動かす
high-torque：高トルク（回転力）
do start：《強調》
Federal Aviation Administration：連邦航空局
certified ～ as …：～を…として認定した
propulsion：推進力
commercial use：商用利用
that：《代名詞で前文を示す》
worked out：解決される
As that process occurs：認可されれば
competitors：競合会社
focused on ～：取り組んでいた
"urban air mobility"：「都会的空間移動、都会空輸」

## Exercises

### Multiple Choice

次の１～５の英文を完成させるために、a～dの中から最も適切なものを１つ選びなさい。

**1.** Electric planes have the advantage of

- **a.** using light batteries.
- **b.** needing very little jet fuel.
- **c.** not emitting carbon.
- **d.** all of the above.

**2.** The Electro plane has the disadvantage of

- **a.** silent propellors.
- **b.** batteries that do not last long.
- **c.** weak lift-off power.
- **d.** seating only one person.

**3.** The writer enjoyed the first part of his flight in the Slovenian plane ＿＿＿＿＿＿ the last part.

- **a.** less than
- **b.** more than
- **c.** as much as
- **d.** as little as

**4.** The Alia can take off and land

- **a.** without a runway.
- **b.** without a battery.
- **c.** only in warm weather.
- **d.** only with the help of a drone.

**5.** The aircraft industry wants e-planes with

- **a.** heavier batteries and better control systems.
- **b.** lighter batteries and higher performance motors.
- **c.** lighter batteries and lower performance motors.
- **d.** heavier batteries and less powerful motors.

## True or False

本文の内容に合致するものにT（True）、合致しないものにF（False）をつけなさい。

(　　) **1.** Electric planes have been discussed ever since humans started flying.

(　　) **2.** E-plane motors need internal combustion engines.

(　　) **3.** The Alia does not emit carbon dioxide.

(　　) **4.** The Slovenian plane can fly for hours without noise.

(　　) **5.** The Federal Aviation Administration is likely to certify commercial e-planes soon.

## Vocabulary

次のクロスワードパズルを、下の Across 横、Down 縦の英文説明を読んで、Unit 20の記事から最も適切な語を見つけ、□の中に1文字ずつ入れなさい。

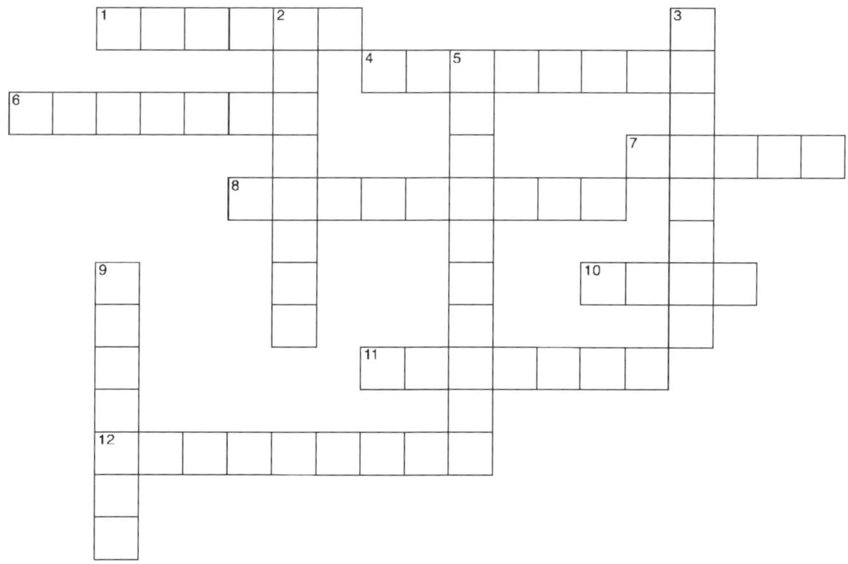

**ACROSS**

**1.** road used by plane to take off and land
**4.** science or business of flying
**6.** person who starts company
**7.** person who flies planes
**8.** initial model or design
**10.** material that produces power
**11.** device that stores electricity
**12.** rotating blades that power plane or boat

**DOWN**

**2.** plane
**3.** person who designs technology
**5.** teacher
**9.** the part of a plane in which the pilot sits

Unit **21**

# ●韓国での「多文化主義」とは

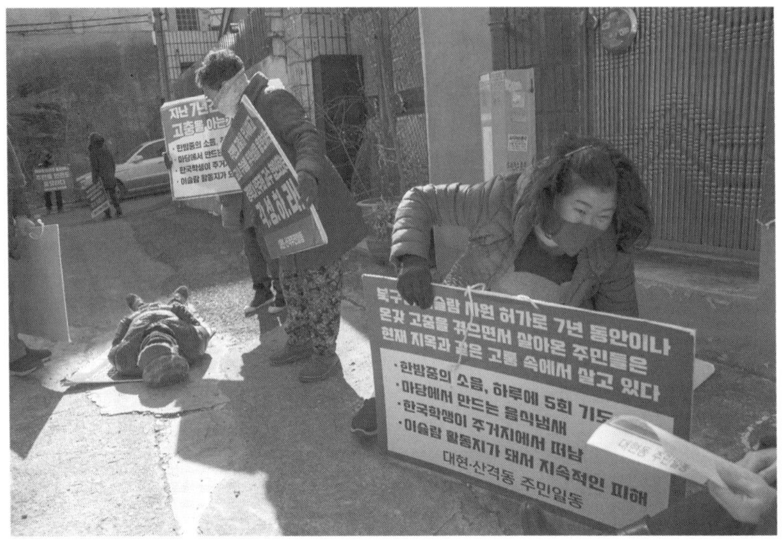


韓国・大邱でイスラム教モスク建設を巡り建築主と地元住民が対立。
「多文化主義」とは？　　The New York Times ／ Redux ／アフロ

## *Before you read*

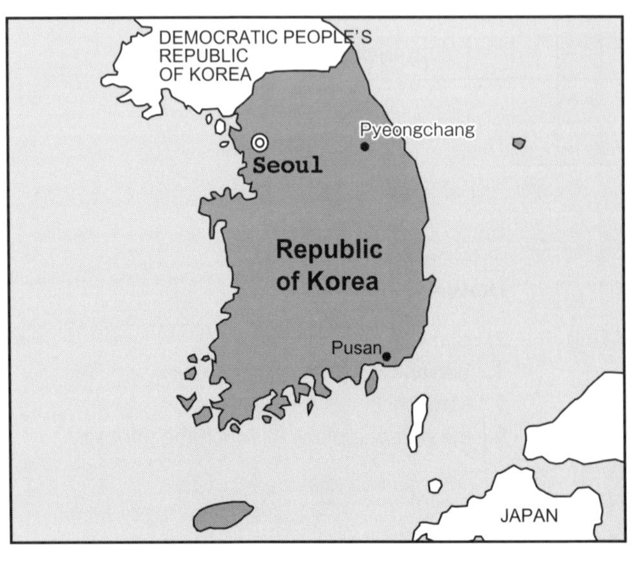


Republic of Korea（South Korea）
大韓民国
38度線を挟み朝鮮民主主義人民共和国の統治区域と対峙する分断国家である

面積　100,210km²（日本の約４分の１）（世界107位）
人口　51,830,000人（世界28位）
民族　大半が朝鮮民族
首都　ソウル
公用語　朝鮮語
宗教　キリスト教・カトリック　20.6%
　　　キリスト教・プロテスタント　34.5%
　　　仏教　42.9%
GDP　１兆6,308億米ドル（世界10位）
　　　１人当たりの GDP　33,320米ドル（世界28位）
通貨　ウォン
政体　民主共和制
識字率　99%

## Words and Phrases

次の１～５の語句の説明として最も近いものをａ～ｅから１つ選び、(　　) 内に記入しなさい。

| | | | |
|---|---|---|---|
| **1.** a den of | (　　) | **a.** the worst or heaviest burden |
| **2.** expose | (　　) | **b.** give protection to |
| **3.** grapple | (　　) | **c.** home to |
| **4.** brunt | (　　) | **d.** reveal |
| **5.** harbor | (　　) | **e.** struggle |

## Summary

次の英文は記事の要約です。下の語群から最も適切な語を１つ選び、(　　) 内に記入しなさい。

2-43

Many Koreans think of themselves as a small nation (　　　　) to maintain their identity. Hence the rise of (　　　　) has made some feel uncomfortable. Islam is often looked at (　　　　), so when Muslims established a mosque in the city of Daegu there was local (　　　　). But because of labor shortages Korea has little choice but to welcome immigrants and treat them (　　　　).

fairly　　hostility　　multiculturalism　　negatively　　struggling

2022年５月10日に第20代大韓民国大統領に就任した尹錫悦（ユン・ソクヨル）は、1960年12月18日に生まれた。ソウル大卒業後、司法試験を受け続け、９回目で合格して検事になった。「権力から独立した検察」を主張し、朴槿恵（パククネ）元大統領をめぐる贈収賄事件を捜査指揮し、2017年に朴氏を逮捕。文政権に評価され、2019年から2021年まで検察総長を務めた。選挙時の公約として掲げた「大統領府の移転」を踏まえ、当選後に韓国の大統領府の名称を「大統領室」に改名し、移転が正式に決定された。移転後の青瓦台の建物と敷地は公園として国民に開放することになった。また、数え年、実年齢、満年齢の３種類の数え方の統一を、法的・社会的にも満年齢を基準とする法改正を2023年までに進める方針も示した。

尹錫悦（ユン・ソクヨル）氏の大統領就任後、これまでの文在寅（ムン・ジェイン）政権時代に悪化した日韓関係を革新系から保守系への政権交代で雪解けにつながるのではないかと期待されている。しかし、政治経験のない検察出身の尹氏の手腕は未知数とされ、国会では野党が過半数を占め、政権運営は簡単ではない。日韓の対立が続いているのは、「元慰安婦」と「元徴用工」の問題である。大統領就任式に出席した林芳正外相は「両国間の懸案の本質的な解決に迅速に取り組む必要がある」とする岸田文雄首相の親書を尹氏に渡したが、問題の解決は容易ではない。

## Reading

2-44

# How 'Multiculturalism' Became a Bad Word in South Korea

DAEGU, South Korea — Inside the dimly lit house, young Muslim men knelt and prayed in silence. Outside, their Korean neighbors gathered with angry signs to protest "a den of terrorists" moving into their neighborhood.

In a densely populated but otherwise quiet district in Daegu, a city in southeastern South Korea, a highly emotional standoff is underway.

2-45

Roughly 150 Muslims, mostly students at the nearby Kyungpook National University, started building a mosque in a lot next door to their temporary house of worship about a year ago. When their Korean neighbors found out, they were furious.

The mosque would turn the neighborhood of Daehyeon-dong into "an enclave of Muslims and a crime-infested slum," the Korean neighbors wrote on signs and protest banners. It would bring more "noise" and a "food smell" from an unfamiliar culture, driving out the Korean residents.

2-46

The fault line between the two communities here has exposed an uncomfortable truth in South Korea. At a time when the country enjoys more global influence than ever — with consumers around the world eager to dance to its music, drive its cars and buy its smartphones — it is also grappling with a fierce wave of anti-immigrant fervor and Islamophobia. While it has successfully exported its culture abroad, it has been slow to welcome other cultures at home.

The mosque dispute has become a flash point, part of a larger phenomenon in which South Koreans have had to confront what it means to live in an increasingly diverse society. Muslims have often borne the brunt of racist misgivings, particularly after the Taliban executed two South Korean missionaries in 2007.

Bad Word：悪口、好ましくない言葉

DAEGU：大邱（テグ）《韓国東南部の内陸にある広域市》

signs：プラカード

den：巣窟

standoff：対立

Kyungpook National University：慶北大学

lot：土地、区画

Daehyeon-dong：デヒョン洞

enclave：居留地

fault line：断層線のようなもの、深刻な意見の相違

grappling with ～：～に取り組む、立ち向かう

Islamophobia：イスラム恐怖症

dispute：紛争

confront ～：～に直面する

borne the brunt of ～：～の矢面に立った

misgivings：不安、疑念

Taliban：タリバン《アフガニスタンのイスラム原理主義組織》

executed ～：～を処刑した

missionaries：（キリスト教）宣教師

2-47

The arrival of 500 Yemeni asylum seekers on the island of Jeju in 2018 triggered South Korea's first series of organized anti-immigrant protests. The government responded to fears that the asylum seekers were harboring terrorists by banning them from leaving the island.

Many Koreans explain their attitude toward foreigners by citing history: their small nation has survived invasions and occupations for centuries, maintaining its territory, language and ethnic identity. Those who oppose the mosque and immigration more broadly have often warned that an influx of foreigners would threaten South Korea's "pure blood" and "ethnic homogeneity."

2-48

Some say the country does not have much of a choice.

South Korea's rise as a cultural powerhouse has coincided with a demographic crisis. Years of low birthrates and rising incomes in urban areas have led to shortages of women who want to marry and live in rural towns. Farms and factories have found it difficult to fill low-wage jobs. Universities lack local students.

To help alleviate the challenges, South Korea opened its doors to workers and students from other nations. Some rural men began to marry foreign women, especially from Vietnam. Yet when the government introduced policies to support "multicultural families," there was a backlash. Suddenly, words like "multiculturalism" and "diversity" became pejorative terms for many South Koreans.

By Choe Sang-Hun
*The New York Times , March 1, 2022*

asylum seekers：亡命希望者
island of Jeju：済州（チェジュ）島
harboring terrorists：隠れテロリスト
occupations：占領
ethnic：民族的
influx：流入
homogeneity：同質性
powerhouse：大国
coincided with ～：～と同時に起きた
demographic：人口動態の
fill jobs：職に就く
local：（地元の）韓国人
alleviate ～：～を緩和する
backlash：反発
pejorative：軽蔑的な

## Exercises

### Multiple Choice

次の１の英文の質問に答え、２～５の英文を完成させるために、ａ～ｄの中から最も適切なものを１つ選びなさい。

**1.** What does Islamophobia mean?

**a.** Attraction to the Muslim religion and culture.
**b.** Fear of the Muslim religion and people.
**c.** Dislike of Muslim art and architecture.
**d.** Fondness for Muslim art and ideas.

**2.** In Daegu, some local Koreans worried that Muslims would create

**a.** loud noise and strange food smells.
**b.** poverty and demographic crisis.
**c.** purity and ethnic homogeneity.
**d.** consumerism and cultural influence.

**3.** While exporting its culture to the world, South Korea has

**a.** warmly embraced other cultures.
**b.** slowly absorbed migrant cultures.
**c.** hardly imported foreign cultures.
**d.** quickly welcomed diverse cultures.

**4.** The arrival in Jeju of 500 asylum seekers from Yemen

**a.** triggered terrorist acts in South Korea.
**b.** helped South Koreans appreciate their global influence.
**c.** increased support for multiculturalism in South Korea.
**d.** led South Koreans to start anti-immigrant protests.

**5.** Koreans' distrust of other cultures could be linked to historical struggles to defend their

**a.** ethnic identity.
**b.** cultural popularity.
**c.** economic expansion.
**d.** demographic diversity.

## True or False

本文の内容に合致するものにT（True）、合致しないものにF（False）をつけなさい。

(　　) **1.** Diversity became a negative word for many South Koreans.

(　　) **2.** According to the writer, foreign women come to South Korea's rural areas because of the nation's cultural attractions.

(　　) **3.** Consumers around the world want to dance to South Korea's music and buy its smartphones.

(　　) **4.** It might be said that South Koreans need foreigners, yet do not want them.

(　　) **5.** Many South Koreans seem to associate Muslims with terrorism.

## Vocabulary

次の英文は、読売新聞の The Japan News「えいご工房」に掲載された *Yoon elected as new South Korean president*『ユン氏、次期韓国大統領に選出』の記事の一部です。下の語群から最も適切なものを１つ選び、(　)内に記入しなさい。

Seoul (AP) — South Korea's President-elect Yoon Sukyeol said on March 10 he would (　　　) an alliance with the United States, build up a powerful military and sternly (　　　) with North Korean provocations, hours after he won the country's (　　　) election to become its next leader.

Yoon, whose single five-year term is to begin in May, said during his campaign he would make a (　　　) alliance with the United States the center of his foreign policy. He's accused outgoing liberal President Moon Jae-in of (　　　) toward Pyongyang and Beijing and away from Washington. He's also stressed the need to recognize the strategic importance of (　　　) ties with Tokyo despite recent bilateral historical disputes.

Some experts say a Yoon government will likely be able to reinforce ties with Washington and improve (　　　) with Tokyo but can't really (　　　) frictions with Pyongyang and Beijing.

| avoid | boosted | cope | hard-fought |
|---|---|---|---|
| relations | repairing | solidify | tilting |

Unit 22

# ●アフリカでクーデター多発の理由

2020年８月18日、マリのバマにある独立広場に反乱軍兵士が到着し、住民たちから歓迎を受ける。その後、大統領と首相は拘束された
AFP／WAA

## Before you read

### Republic of Guinea　ギニア共和国

**面積**　245,857km²（本州とほぼ同じ）／**首都**　コナクリ
**公用語**　フランス語／**人口**　12,770,000人
**宗教**　イスラム教、キリスト教／**民族**　プル、マリンケ
**識字率**　57%／**通貨**　ギニア・フラン／**政体**　共和制
GDP　135.9億ドル／１人当たりのGNI　950ドル

### Burkina Faso　ブルキナ・ファソ

**面積**　274,200km²（日本の70%）／**首都**　ワガドゥグ
**公用語**　フランス語／**人口**　20,900,000人
**宗教**　伝統宗教　57%、イスラム教　31%、キリスト教　12%
**民族**　モシ、グルマンチェ／**識字率**　57%／**通貨**　CFAフラン
**政体**　共和制／GDP　173.7億ドル／１人当たりのGNI　790ドル

### Republic of Chad　チャド共和国

**面積**　1,284,000km²（日本の3.4倍）／**首都**　ンジャメナ
**公用語**　フランス語、アラビア語／**民族**　サラ、チャド・アラブ
**人口**　20,250,000人／**宗教**　イスラム教　52%　キリスト教　44%
**識字率**　34%／**通貨**　CFAフラン／**政体**　共和制
GDP　108.4億ドル／１人当たりのGNI　660ドル

### Republic of Mali　マリ共和国

**面積**　1,240,000km²（日本の3.3倍）／**首都**　バマコ
**公用語**　フランス語／**人口**　20,250,000人
**宗教**　イスラム教　80%、キリスト教／**民族**　バンバラ、プル
**識字率**　61%／**通貨**　CFAフラン／**政体**　共和制
GDP　173.9億ドル／１人当たりのGNI　830ドル

### Republic of Niger　ニジェール共和国

**面積**　1,267,000km²（日本の3.3倍）／**首都**　ニアメ
**公用語**　フランス語／**人口**　24,210,000人
**宗教**　イスラム教・スンニ派　90%／**民族**　ハウサ、ジェルマ
**識字率**　35%／**通貨**　CFAフラン／**政体**　共和制
GDP　136.8億ドル／１人当たりのGNI　540ドル

### The Republic of the Sudan　スーダン共和国

**面積**　1,880,000km²（日本の約５倍）／**首都**　ハルツーム
**公用語**　アラビア語／**人口**　42,810,000人
**宗教**　イスラム教、キリスト教／**民族**　アラブ人、ヌビア人
**識字率**　69%／**通貨**　スーダン・ポンド／**政体**　共和制
GDP　189億ドル／１人当たりのGNI　590ドル

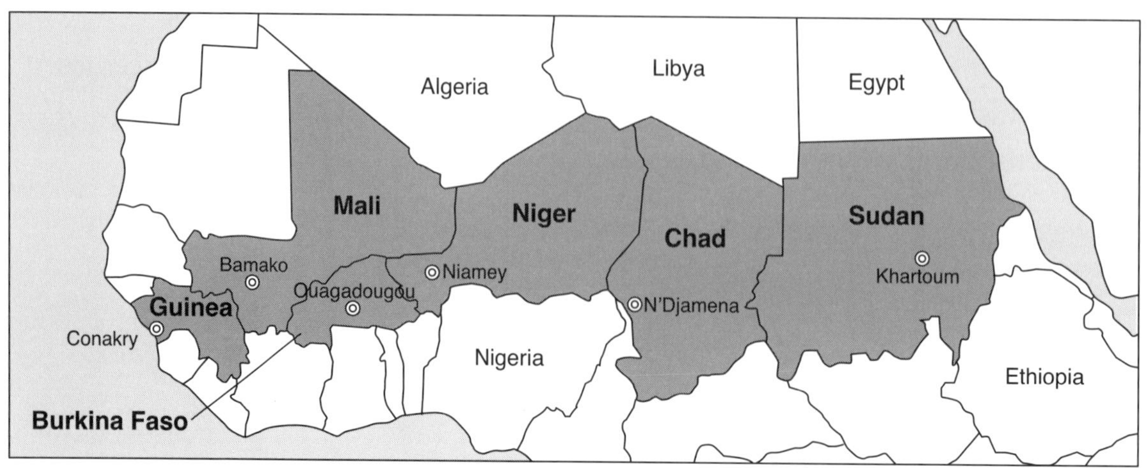

## Words and Phrases

次の１～５の語句の説明として最も近いものをａ～ｅから１つ選び、(　　) 内に記入しなさい。

| | | | |
|---|---|---|---|
| **1.** ring out | (　　) | **a.** large area | |
| **2.** dissolve | (　　) | **b.** keep hold of | |
| **3.** cling to | (　　) | **c.** easily spread | |
| **4.** contagious | (　　) | **d.** echo | |
| **5.** swath | (　　) | **e.** close | |

## Summary

次の英文は記事の要約です。下の語群から最も適切な語を１つ選び、(　　) 内に記入しなさい。

Military coups (　　　) governments in five African nations in just one
2-49 and a half years. The (　　　) was in Mali in August, 2020. Then came Chad, (　　　) by Guinea, Sudan and Burkina Faso. There was also an (　　　) coup in Niger. Some people think that if no action is taken against these (　　　) regimes there will be more takeovers in the region.

attempted　　first　　followed　　illegal　　unseated

アフリカのサハラ砂漠南縁部に広がるサヘル地域の情勢悪化が深刻だ。イスラム過激派の「アルカイダ」の関連組織 JNIM と「イラク・レバントのイスラム国」の ISIL が活動を活発化させている。JNIM は、活動地域等をめぐり ISIL と戦闘を交えている。旧宗主国のフランスは、過激派掃討作戦を続けているが、根絶はかなり難しい。イスラム過激派の台頭は、2011年のリビアのカダフィ政権の崩壊がきっかけとなった。マリに帰国した遊牧民トゥアレグの傭兵の武装蜂起に乗じて過激派が力を蓄え、周辺のブルキナファソ、ニジェールなどの周辺国にも広がった。

マリでは、2020年８月以降、２度に渡り軍事クーデターが起きた。22年の１月に、ブルキナファソでは親仏派の大統領に対し反乱軍がクーデターを成功させた。ニジェールでは住民虐殺が止まらず、ナイジェリア、チャド、カメルーンでは「ボコ・ハラム」や「イスラム国」系組織が横行している。サヘルを立て直そうと2013年からフランスは軍事介入を始めたが、土着化したイスラム過激派の力を排除することは困難だ。マリは、ロシアを頼り、プーチン政権に近い民間軍事会社と契約した。サヘルは、地中海沿岸諸国とサハラ以南のアフリカ各国とのつなぎ地域にあたる。混乱をこのままにしておくと、周辺諸国に波及し、欧州への移民や難民が増える恐れがある。

## Reading

2-50

# Five African countries. Six coups. Why now?

Gunfire rings out. Rumors spread of a military takeover. The president is nowhere to be seen. The nation turns on the television and collectively switches to the state channel, where they see new leaders, wearing berets and fatigues, announce that the constitution has been suspended, national assembly dissolved, borders closed.

In the past 18 months, in similar scenes, military leaders have toppled the governments of Mali, Chad, Guinea, Sudan and now, Burkina Faso. West African leaders Friday called an emergency summit on the situation in Burkina Faso, at which the new military leader, Lt. Col. Paul-Henri Damiba, told the nation in his first public address Thursday night that he would return the country to constitutional order "when the conditions are right."

2-51

The resurgence of coups has alarmed the region's remaining civilian leaders. Ghana's president, Nana Akufo-Addo, said Friday, "It represents a threat to peace, security and stability in West-Africa."

These five nations that have recently experienced military coups form a broken line that stretches across the wide bulge of Africa, from Guinea on the west coast to Sudan in the east.

First came Mali, in August 2020. The military took advantage of public anger at a stolen parliamentary election and the government's failure to protect its people from violent extremists, and arrested President Ibrahim Boubacar Keita and forced him to resign on state television. Mali actually had two coups in a nine-month span.

2-52

An unusual coup unfolded in Chad in April 2021. A president who had ruled for three decades was killed on the battlefield, and his son was quickly installed in his place — a violation of the constitution.

In March 2021, there was a failed coup attempt in Niger,

coups：クーデター、政変
takeover：乗っ取り、権力奪取
berets：ベレー帽
fatigues：戦闘服
constitution：憲法
suspended：停止された
national assembly：国会
dissolved：解散された
called ～：～を召集した
Lt. Col.：中佐
public address：国民に向けた演説
"when the conditions are right"：「条件が整えば」
resurgence：再流行
broken line：破線
bulge：膨らみ
took advantage of ～：～を利用した
parliamentary：議会の
extremists：過激派
resign：辞任する
unfolded：起きた
installed in ～：～に任命された

then in September 2021, it was Guinea's turn: A high-ranking officer trained by the United States overthrew a president who had tried to cling to power. Then in October, it was Sudan's: The country's top generals seized power, tearing up a power-sharing deal that was supposed to lead to the country's first free election in decades.

2-53

That's more than 114 million people now ruled by soldiers who have illegally seized power. There were four successful coups in Africa in 2021 — there hadn't been that many in a single calendar year since 1999. United Nations Secretary-General Antonio Guterres called it "an epidemic of coup d'etats."

Coups are contagious. When the Malian government fell, analysts warned that Burkina Faso could follow. Now that it has, they're warning that if the coup plotters aren't punished, there will be more coups in the region.

2-54

People are fed up with their governments for many reasons — major security threats, relentless humanitarian disasters and millions of young people having no prospects.

Governments are performing abysmally, said Abdul Zanya Salifu, a scholar at the University of Calgary in Alberta, Canada, who focuses on the Sahel, the swath of Africa that lies just below the Sahara. So, he said, the military thinks: "You know, why not take over?"

By Ruth Maclean

*The New York Times, January 31, 2022*

generals：将軍
seized power：権力を掌握した
tearing up ～：～を破棄する
power-sharing deal：権限分割協定
Secretary-General：事務総長
epidemic：流行
contagious：伝染する
plotters：首謀者
fed up with ～：～にうんざりしている
humanitarian：人道的
prospects：将来の見通し
Sahel：サヘル《サハラ砂漠南縁にある地域》
swath：帯状の土地

## *Exercises*

### Multiple Choice

次の１～５の英文を完成させるために、a～dの中から最も適切なものを１つ選びなさい。

**1.** The governments of Mali, Chad, Guinea, Sudan and Burkina Faso

**a.** were recently overthrown by military leaders.
**b.** have launched military attacks on neighboring countries.
**c.** have recently experienced failed coups.
**d.** are clinging to power despite attempted coups.

**2.** Nana Akufo-Addo believes the military takeovers

**a.** represent constitutional order.
**b.** indicate peaceful political transition.
**c.** threaten African stability.
**d.** resulted in African security.

**3.** In April 2021, the president who had ruled Chad for thirty years

**a.** was arrested.
**b.** was killed.
**c.** launched a coup.
**d.** put his son in power.

**4.** The UN Secretary-General

**a.** warned Africans that they would get ill.
**b.** said the coups would never stop.
**c.** criticized Africa's health policies.
**d.** compared the events to a disease.

**5.** Many young Africans are sick of governments that seem to offer them

**a.** successive takeovers.
**b.** hope for change.
**c.** no future.
**d.** military power.

## True or False

本文の内容に合致するものにＴ（True)、合致しないものにＦ（False）をつけなさい。

( ) **1.** The military coups began in the north of Africa and ended in the south.

( ) **2.** The first in this string of coups occurred in Mali.

( ) **3.** In Guinea, an American-trained officer overthrew the president.

( ) **4.** Over the last two decades Africa has experienced about four coups every year.

( ) **5.** Abdul Zanya Salifu says African military figures often feel they can perform better than civilian leaders.

## Vocabulary

次の１～８は、アフリカのサヘル諸国に関する英文です。下記の国名から１つ選び（ ）内に、そして、地図からａ～ｈを選び［ ］内に記入しなさい。

**1.** ( ) has borders with Libya, Niger, Nigeria, Cameroon, Central African Republic and Sudan, and its capital is Ndjamena. [ ]

**2.** ( ) is a country in eastern Africa and its capital is Khartoum. [ ]

**3.** ( )'s capital is Bamako and its main language is French. [ ]

**4.** ( ) is a small country and has borders with Djibouti, Ethiopia and Sudan. [ ]

**5.** ( ) is a large republic in western Africa facing the Gulf of Guinea. [ ]

**6.** ( )'s currency is called the Guinean franc. [ ]

**7.** ( ) is a country south of Mali and its capital is Ouagadougou. [ ]

**8.** ( ) has borders with Libya, Algeria, Mali, Burkina Faso, Benin, Nigeria and Chad. [ ]

| Burkina Faso | Chad | Eritrea | Guinea |
|---|---|---|---|
| Mali | Niger | Nigeria | Sudan |

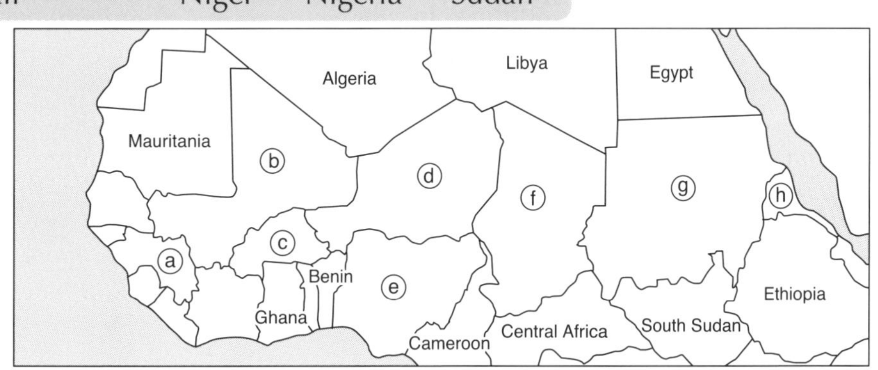

# Unit 23

## ●リオのカーニバルのパレードを巡り争い騒ぎ

ブラジルのリオデジャネイロ市当局がストリート系サンバチーム「ブロコス」のカーニバル参加を禁止すると、2022年4月13日、それに抗議して、街中でサンバを踊る市民たち　AP／アフロ

## *Before you read*

Federative Republic of Brazil
ブラジル連邦共和国

面積　8,512,000km²（日本の22.5倍）（世界5位）
人口　209,470,000人（世界6位）
民族　ヨーロッパ系　48%、アフリカ系　8%
　　　アジア系　1.1%、混血　43%
　　　先住民　0.4%
首都　ブラジリア
最大都市　サンパウロ
公用語　ポルトガル語
宗教　キリスト教・カトリック　65%
　　　キリスト教・プロテスタント　22%
　　　無宗教　8%
GDP　1兆8,850億米ドル
　　　1人当たりのGNI　9,080米ドル
通貨　レアル
政体　連邦共和制
識字率　93.2%

## Words and Phrases

次の1～5の語句の説明として最も近いものをa～eから1つ選び、(　　)内に記入しなさい。

1. riotous (　　)
2. shindig (　　)
3. glitter-smeared (　　)
4. plead for (　　)
5. brandish (　　)

a. party
b. carry
c. demand or ask desperately
d. covered in decorations
e. chaotic and noisy

## Summary

次の英文は記事の要約です。下の語群から最も適切な語を1つ選び、(　　)内に記入しなさい。

2-55

After being (　　　) for two years, Rio's carnival will take place in the Sambódromo stadium. Some private events will also be (　　　). But the colorful street parades have not been (　　　) permission to return as the city authorities claim there has been insufficient time to prepare. In addition to being (　　　), many local groups feel (　　　) against.

allowed　　cancelled　　disappointed　　discriminated　　given

リオデジャネイロのカーニバル（Carnaval do Rio de Janeiro）は、復活祭前の40日間に及ぶ四旬節の期間に入る前に行われる世界最大規模の祭りである。パレードとサンバ、打楽器の演奏が結び付いたカーニバルは、「地上最大のショー」とも言われている。その歴史は、1723年にまで遡る。ダンスは、かつて奴隷たちがアフリカからもたらされ、都市の外縁部の貧しい集落で人気のあるサンバである。バトゥカーダという、主に打楽器演奏を基盤にした音楽で、リオのカーニバルにはなくてはならないものである。この音楽は、「歌いながら、踊りながら、パレードすることを可能にするようなリズムが必要とされて、誕生したものである」。パレードは賞金付きコンテスト形式になっており審査が行われる。観客席が設けられ、約6万人のダンサーを約150万人の観客が見る。

「リオのカーニバル」は、ブラジルのリオデジャネイロで毎年夏に開かれるが、2021年は新型コロナウイルスの影響で史上初めて中止となり、今年2022年もオミクロン株の感染拡大で、当初2月下旬に予定されていた開催が、2か月延期された。およそ2年ぶりの開催となったカーニバルは、4月22日夜、12のグルーポ・エスペシャル・チームが歌やダンスの美しさなどを披露した。熱気が最高潮を迎えた。それぞれのチームは2500人から最大3600人のメンバーで構成され、華麗な衣装を身につけたダンサーたちが、大がかりな山車とともに、特別会場に設けられた700メートルの花道を行進した。中央の打楽器隊だけでも200人から250人で編成されている。コンテストは、名門 Grande Rio が優勝、Beija Flor が準優勝を飾った。ブラジルでは、新型コロナウイルスに感染して68万人が亡くなっている。

## Reading

2-56

# Rio carnival groups fight for right to party ahead of official celebrations

Rio's world-famous samba schools will return to action next week for their first parades at the Sambódromo stadium in more than two years. But the carnival enthusiasts behind hundreds of "*blocos*" — riotous musical troupes that roam the streets clutching brass instruments and booze — are furious they have not received authorization to gather.

2-57

The Omicron variant scuppered plans for this year's pre-Lenten carnival, which should have been held in late February. But while the Sambódromo competition was rearranged for next weekend — and often expensive private shindigs are also taking place — authorities claim there was insufficient time to prepare for the free outdoor blocos, which attract hundreds of thousands of partygoers.

More than 120 blocos denounced their sidelining this week in a manifesto that declared: "The streets belong to the people and we are free to speak."

Hundreds of glitter-smeared carnival activists pranced through downtown Rio on Wednesday night to protest what they called a hammer-blow to the local economy and one of Brazil's most important cultural treasures.

2-58

"The city hall has abandoned street carnival," complained Kiko Horta, a founder of one of Rio's best-known blocos, the Cordão do Boitatá.

"It makes no sense. Street carnival — along with the [Sambódromo] carnival — is the city's most important festival. It has tremendous symbolic, cultural and economic value. Simply forbidding it is absurd," Horta added.

Telma Neves, the president of the samba bloco Engata no Centro (City Centre Coupling), joined the demo with her 83-year-old mother Georgina who had not missed a carnival since she was six. "We've spent the last two years in silence,

Rio：リオデジャネイロ《ブラジルの都市》
carnival：カーニバル、謝肉祭《カトリック国で四旬節（Lent）の断食に入る直前に行われる祭り》
party：どんちゃん騒ぎをする
first ～ in more than two years：２年ぶりの～
"*blocos*"：「ブロコス」《ストリートカーニバル・グループ》
troupes：一座、一行
brass instruments：金管楽器
booze：酒
authorization：許可
Omicron variant：オミクロン変異株《新型コロナウイルスの変異株》
pre-Lenten：四旬節前の
shindigs：大騒ぎ
sidelining：傍観者にされたこと
glitter-smeared：キラキラに染まった
pranced through ～：～を跳ね回った
Cordão do Boitatá：ボイタタ（火蛇）グループ
absurd：馬鹿げてる
Engata no Centro：エンガタ・ノ・セントロ《都心連合（結）》
missed ～：～を休んだ

unable to do anything," Neves, 58, complained. "We're pleading for the right to our own carnival."

2-59

Wednesday's rally offered a snapshot of the weird and wonderful world of Rio street carnival, as bacchanals of all ages and from all walks of life danced through town wearing a dizzying medley of costumes — or in some cases almost no clothes at all.

rally：集会

bacchanals：どんちゃん騒ぎをする人《バッカス神が語源》

all walks of life：あらゆる職業や地位の人々

One man came dressed as a grim reaper brandishing a Minion toy and a pretend syringe — a political critique of President Jair Bolsonaro's denialist response to Covid.

grim reaper：死神

Minion：ミニオン《映画キャラクター；最強最悪の人物に使える（この場合は大統領が死神を暗示）》

Claudio Manhães, a 43-year-old x-ray technician, came to represent his group — founded by a gang of samba-loving radiology professionals and called Te Vejo Por Dentro, or I Can See Your Insides. "We thought this year's carnival would be a super carnival like in 1919 after the Spanish flu," Manhães said, showing off photographs of the green T-shirts his bloco had printed for a party that would no longer take place.

denialist：否認主義者の

Covid：コロナウイルス感染症

radiology professionals：放射線学専門家

Spanish flu：スペイン風邪《世界で2,000万人から4,000万人が死亡したとされる》

showing off ～：～を見せびらかす

2-60

"It's sad. There were so many expectations," Manhães sighed.

expectations：期待

Tarcísio Motta, a leftist councillor who has criticised the government's treatment of the blocos, questioned whether Rio's mayor wanted to cast himself as "an enemy of carnival". "The city hall is right to support the samba schools ... but why haven't they done the same for street carnival?" Motta asked, accusing authorities of depriving residents of their legal right to carnival.

councillor：議員

accusing ～ of …：～が…したと非難する

depriving ～ of …：～から…を奪う

By Tom Phillips

*The Guardian News & Media Ltd, April 14, 2022*

## Exercises

### Multiple Choice

次の１～５の英文を完成させるために、a～dの中から最も適切なものを１つ選びなさい。

**1.** ____________________, but street activists and enthusiasts haven't received permission to get together.

**a.** Rio's tango groups will be able to return to action
**b.** Rio's samba schools will return to action
**c.** Rio's "blocos" have been invited to parade
**d.** Rio's carnival will be just how it was before the pandemic

**2.** Plans for the pre-Lenten carnival in late February, 2022,

**a.** were postponed until the following weekend.
**b.** were implemented despite the pandemic.
**c.** were discontinued because of the Omicron variant.
**d.** were halted by a flu outbreak.

**3.** Rio's street carnival has been

**a.** of economic as well as cultural significance.
**b.** forbidden for many years.
**c.** held inside a stadium for the last two years.
**d.** of little interest to Brazilians for a long time.

**4.** Telma Neves' mother Georgina ____________________ since she was six.

**a.** had not joined a carnival
**b.** had not missed a carnival
**c.** had not experienced a carnival
**d.** had not prohibited a carnival

**5.** Claudio Manhães had hoped this year's carnival would be

**a.** an extraordinary one like in 1919 after Covid-19.
**b.** an exceptional one like in 2008 after the financial crisis.
**c.** a superb one like in 1991 after the influenza outbreak.
**d.** a super one like in 1919 after the Spanish flu.

## True or False

本文の内容に合致するものにT（True）、合致しないものにF（False）をつけなさい。

( ) **1.** The city hall in Rio de Janeiro gave its support to street carnival.

( ) **2.** Carnival enthusiasts have spent the last two years performing.

( ) **3.** Carnival participants usually dance to brass bands on the streets.

( ) **4.** Street carnival in Brazil has symbolic, cultural and economic value.

( ) **5.** Telma Neves is president of the samba bloco Te Vejo Por Dentro.

## Vocabulary

次の（1）～（6）はキリスト教のカトリックの年中行事です。該当する英語説明文を下のa～fの中から1つ選び（ ）内に、そして行事を時系列に並べ、[ ] 内に2～6までの順番を入れなさい。

**(1)** Ash Wednesday ( ) [ ]
**(2)** Carnival ( ) [ 1 ]
**(3)** Christmas ( ) [ ]
**(4)** Easter ( ) [ ]
**(5)** Lent ( ) [ ]
**(6)** Mardi Gras ( ) [ ]

**a.** a Christian holy day in March or April when Christians remember the death of Christ and his return to life

**b.** the day before the first day of Lent

**c.** the day when Christians celebrate the birth of Christ

**d.** the 40 days before Easter, during which Christians customarily eat less food

**e.** the first day of Lent, when some Christians put ashes on their foreheads as a sign of Penitence

**f.** public dancing, eating, drinking, processions and shows held in Roman Catholic countries in the weeks before Lent

Unit 24

# ●ビゴレクシア（筋肉醜形恐怖症）とは

プロテインを持つボディビルダー。若い男性の憧れ？　　アフロ

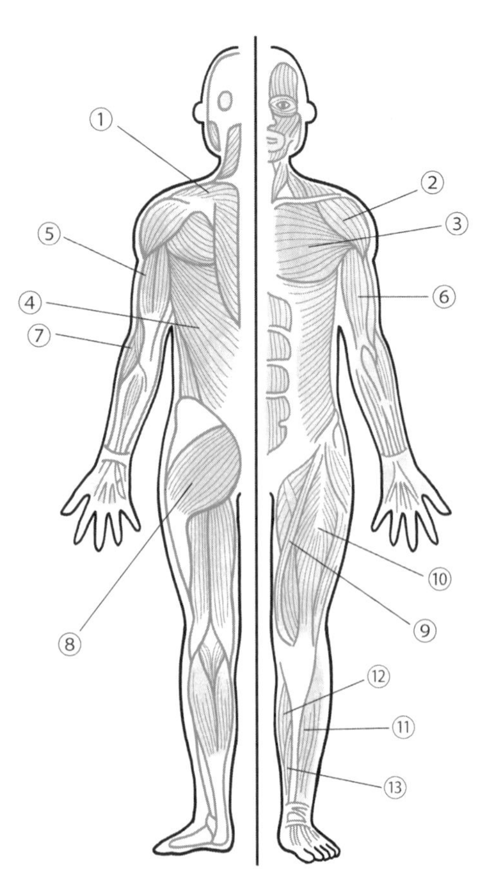


## *Before you read*

**a.** Biceps（上腕二頭筋） [　　]
**b.** Brachioradialis（腕とう骨筋） [　　]
**c.** Deltoid（三角筋） [　　]
**d.** Gastrocnemius（ひふく筋） [　　]
**e.** Gluteus maximus（大殿筋） [　　]
**f.** Latissimus dorsi（広背筋） [　　]
**g.** Pectoralis major（大胸筋） [　　]
**h.** Rectus（大腿直筋） [　　]
**i.** Sartorius（縫工筋） [　　]
**j.** Soleus（ひらめ筋） [　　]
**k.** Tibialis anterior（前脛骨筋） [　　]
**l.** Trapezius（僧帽筋） [　　]
**m.** Triceps brachii（上腕三頭筋） [　　]

## Words and Phrases

次の１～５の語句の説明として最も近いものをａ～ｅから１つ選び、（　）内に記入しなさい。

| | | | |
|---|---|---|---|
| **1.** whip into shape | (　　) | **a.** | impossible to reach |
| **2.** fall behind on | (　　) | **b.** | full of muscles |
| **3.** unattainable | (　　) | **c.** | train and improve |
| **4.** beefcake-saturated | (　　) | **d.** | fail to keep up with |
| **5.** mesomorphic | (　　) | **e.** | compact and muscular |

## Summary

次の英文は記事の要約です。下の語群から最も適切な語を１つ選び、（　）内に記入しなさい。

2-61

Research shows that young women can be harmed by social media's (　　　) with body image. However, young men may become (　　　) too. One 16-year-old spends almost as much time (　　　) images of himself on TikTok as he does (　　　) out. With 400,000 followers he seems happy, but other boys might experience anxiety when (　　　) themselves with him.

comparing　　obsessed　　obsession　　posting　　working

ビゲレクシア（Bigorexia）は、身体が小さすぎる、または筋肉が不足しているという考えに執着する筋肉醜形恐怖症として定義されている。外観への執着、ミラーチェック、食事と栄養補助食品の固定、関連する薬物療法とステロイドの使用、気分の落ち込みや怒りにつながる外見への不満が特徴だと言われている。筋肉隆々としているのに、何時間も鏡の前に立ち、体のあらゆる部分を調べ、筋肉量を欠いている細い男しか見えない。同じことが拒食症の女性にも当てはまる。鏡を見ると、骸骨のように痩身なのに、まだ太っていると思っている。この病気の主な原因は、その外観に対する不満の高まりで、治療を必要とする精神障害である。

ステロイドの定期的な使用は中毒性があるため、悪循環から抜け出すことは困難だ。サプリメント（ステロイドまたはホルモン）を使用すると、肝臓がんや肺がんを含む多くの病気の発症を引き起こす。その結果、前立腺肥大または女性化乳房と精子の質の低下が起こる。腎臓や肝臓に永久的な損傷を与えるものもあり、動脈硬化症の変化を増加させるため、心臓発作や脳卒中が頻繁に起こる。神経性食欲不振症も身体醜形障害の一種だ。ジムで何時間も過ごしたり、体の限界をはるかに超えて押したり、戻ってやり直さなければならないと感じたりする。翌日体重を減らし、終わらない筋肉を追加するための食事療法に従う。自分の体を嫌い、身体部分を欠点のように感じる。治療せずに放置すると、強迫性障害が悪化し、ステロイドの誤用やうつ病を引き起こす可能性がある。

## Reading

2-62

# What Is 'Bigorexia'?

Like many high school athletes,Bobby, 16, a junior from Long Island, has spent years whipping his body into shape through protein diets and workouts.

Between rounds of Fortnite and homework, Bobby goes online to study bodybuilders like Greg Doucette, a 46-year-old fitness personality who has more than 1.3 million YouTube subscribers. Bobby also hits his local gym as frequently as six days a week.

2-63

He makes sure to hit the fridge, too, grazing on protein-packed Kodiak Cakes and muscle-mass-building Oreo shakes. He consumes so much protein that classmates sometimes gawk at him for eating upward of eight chicken-and-rice meals at school.

But Bobby isn't getting buff so he can stand out during varsity tryouts. His goal is to compete in a different arena: TikTok.

Bobby now posts his own workout TikToks. Shot on his iPhone 11, usually at the gym or in his family's living room, the videos are devoted to topics like how to get a "gorilla chest," "Popeye forearms" or "Lil Uzi's abs."

Bobby said that he has occasionally fallen behind on his schoolwork because he dedicates so much time to weight lifting and prepping high-protein meals.

2-64

"When Bobby first started posting his videos, our family did not even know what he was doing for months, as he was extremely independent and did stuff on his own," said his father, 49, who is a correctional officer at Rikers Island.

Bobby's father can, in some ways, relate. "When I was younger, I remember seeing the men's fashion magazines and seeing the jacked, buff guys on there and wanted to look like them," he said. "It took me a while to realize that those men's bodies were most likely unattainable."

'Bigorexia'：「ビゴレクシア（筋肉醜形恐怖症）」《自分の体が実際にはたくましいのに貧弱ではないかと慢性的に不安に思ってしまう精神障害》

Long Island：ロング・アイランド《ニューヨーク都市圏に含まれる島》

whipping ～ into shape：～を鍛えて希望通りの形に仕上げる

Fortnite：フォートナイト《バトルロワイアル形式のオンラインゲーム》

personality：有名人

subscribers：加入者

hits ～：～に立ち寄る

Kodiak Cakes：コディアック・ケーキ《パンケーキ製造会社》

Oreo shakes：オレオのミルクセーキ《オレオはクッキーで有名》

upward of ～：～を超える

getting buff：マッチョになる

varsity tryouts：高校代表チーム選手選抜試験

devoted to ～：～をテーマにしている

"Lil Uzi's abs"：「リル・ウージーの腹筋」《大富豪のラッパー》

did stuff：何でもした

correctional officer：刑務官、看守

Rikers Island：ライカーズ島《ニューヨーク市内イースト・リバーの中洲の島で州の主要な刑務所がある》

relate：理解する

jacked：非常に良く発達した筋肉を持った

2-65

But unlike his father's experience, as Bobby's body mass grows, so does his online audience. "Young guys see me as their idol," said Bobby, who has more than 400,000 followers on TikTok. "They want to be just like me, someone who gained muscle as a teenager."

For many boys and young men, muscle worship has become practically a digital rite of passage in today's beefcake-saturated culture. Examples are everywhere — the hypermasculine video games they play, the mesomorphic superheroes in the movies they watch. The top grossing films of last year were ruled by C.G.I.-enhanced masculine clichés: Spider-Man, Shang Chi, Venom and the entire Marvel universe.

2-66

Many doctors and researchers say that the relentless online adulation of muscular male bodies can have a toxic effect on the self-esteem of young men, with the never-ending scroll of six packs and boy-band faces making them feel inadequate and anxious.

And while there has been increased public awareness about how social media can be harmful to teenagers — spurred in part by the leak of internal research from Facebook showing that the company hid the negative effects of Instagram — much of that focus has been on girls.

Recent reports, however, have found that those same online pressures can also cause teenage boys to feel bad about their bodies.

By Alex Hawgood
*The New York Times, March 5, 2022*

body mass：体重

someone：《同格なので前に「つまり」を置く》

rite of passage：通過儀礼

beefcake：男性肉体美

～-saturated：～で飽和した、溢れかえった

hypermasculine：超男性的な

mesomorphic：頑丈な筋肉のがっしりした体質を持つ

top grossing：最高の興行収益を上げた

C.G.I.：コンピュータ生成画像

clichés：定型

Marvel universe：《アメリカン・コミックの老舗出版社マーベル・コミックス社の作品を映画化した世界》

adulation：誇大な賞賛

self-esteem：自尊心

six packs：シックス・パック《鍛えられた腹筋によって六つに分かれて見える腹部》

boy-band：男性アイドルグループの

feel inadequate：無力だと感じる

feel bad：不快感を覚える

## Exercises

### Multiple Choice

次の1～2の英文の質問に答え、3～5の英文を完成させるために、a～dの中から最も適切なものを1つ選びなさい。

**1.** What is 'Bigorexia'?

**a.** A health condition causing someone to think constantly about muscle.
**b.** A mental condition causing someone continually to be on a diet.
**c.** A physical condition making people obsessed with gymnastics.
**d.** A spiritual condition making people want to stay in good health.

**2.** What is beefcake-saturated culture?

**a.** A diet based on the consumption of beef.
**b.** A lifestyle centered on muscle-appreciation.
**c.** An interest in cooking and baking.
**d.** An obsession with superheroes in the movies.

**3.** Bobby has been training to

**a.** remain slim through protein diets and workouts.
**b.** become strong by reducing his food intake.
**c.** build his body through protein diets and workouts.
**d.** increase his body mass by only drinking shakes.

**4.** Many doctors say that the online admiration of muscular males

**a.** can lead young men to try detoxification diets.
**b.** can have a toxic effect on young men's self-worth.
**c.** can lead to toxic waste in boys' bodies.
**d.** can make boys treat each other toxically.

**5.** The online pressures can make boys

**a.** feel good about their bodies.
**b.** get tired of the hours they spend at the gym.
**c.** become bored with their bodies.
**d.** grow anxious about their physical appearance.

## True or False

本文の内容に合致するものにＴ（True）、合致しないものにＦ（False）をつけなさい。

(　　) **1.** Bobby spends hours at the gym every single day.

(　　) **2.** Bobby has sometimes failed to keep up with his schoolwork.

(　　) **3.** Many boys and young men watch the strong masculine superheroes in the movies.

(　　) **4.** When Bobby's father was young, he too would hit his local gym.

(　　) **5.** Fitness personality Greg Doucette has over 1.5 million YouTube subscribers.

## Vocabulary

次の１～８は、「筋トレ」に関する英文です。日本文に合わせて、適切な語を下の語群から１つ選び、(　) 内に記入しなさい。

**1.** １週間に４回ジムに通って、筋トレしている。
I go to the gym and (　　　　) four times a week.

**2.** 引き締まった身体だね。
You have a (　　　　) body.

**3.** ジムに入りびたっていた。
I was one of the gym (　　　　).

**4.** 上腕二頭筋を鍛えるため、ダンベル運動をやっている。
I've been doing dumbbell exercises to strengthen my (　　　　).

**5.** 腹筋見て！６つに割れたよ！
Look at my (　　　　) muscles! I got a six-pack!

**6.** 帰宅後、毎日腕立て伏せをやっている。
I do (　　　　) every day after I get home.

**7.** 腹筋よりストレッチの方が好きだ。
I prefer stretching rather than (　　　　).

**8.** 体脂肪率を下げるのに一番良い方法は何ですか？
What is the most efficient way to get (　　　　)?

| | | | |
|---|---|---|---|
| abdominal | biceps | push-ups | rats |
| shredded | sit-ups | toned | work out |

Unit **25**

# ●日本映画『ドライブ・マイカー』が米アカデミー賞受賞

第94回米アカデミー賞で日本映画「ドライブ・マイカー」が最優秀国際長編映画賞を受賞し、オスカー像を掲げる濱口竜介監督　AFP／WAA

## *Before you read*

### Questions

1. What do you think the article will be about?

   この記事は何の話題についてだと思いますか？

2. What is your favorite Japanese movie? Why?

   あなたの大好きな邦画は何ですか？　なぜ好きなのですか？

## Words and Phrases

次の１～５の語の説明として最も近いものをａ～ｅから１つ選び、(　　) 内に記入しなさい。

**1.** undeterred (　　)
**2.** premier (　　)
**3.** grief (　　)
**4.** prospects (　　)
**5.** accelerate (　　)

**a.** future chances or possibilities
**b.** sadness for someone or something lost
**c.** hold the first official showing
**d.** continuing undisturbed
**e.** do something with increasing speed

## Summary

次の英文は記事の要約です。下の語群から最も適切な語を１つ選び、(　　) 内に記入しなさい。

2-67

Based on a short story by Haruki Murakami, "Drive My Car" is a long film about (　　　). Three major U.S. critics groups (　　　) it best picture, making it the first non-English language one to be recognized as (　　　). But its length and (　　　) may have made the Oscar Academy reluctant to do the same. (　　　), it got the Academy Award for best international picture.

content　grief　instead　such　voted

映画界の最大の祭典、第94回米アカデミー賞の受賞式が、2022年３月27日に行われ、濱口竜介監督の『ドライブ・マイカー』が、最優秀国際長編映画賞を受賞した。世界92か国・地域から出品された映画の頂点に立った。作品賞、監督賞、脚色賞にもノミネートされたが、受賞は叶わなかった。昨21年７月のカンヌ国際映画祭で脚本賞を受賞している。『ドライブ・マイカー』は、村上春樹の短編小説が原作で、妻を失った舞台演出家とつらい過去を持つ寡黙な専属運転手と出会い、互いに再生していく姿を感動的に描いている。上映時間が２時間59分と長いが、繊細な演出、村上春樹の原作の巧みな脚色、見る人の想像力を刺激する点に高い評価を受けた。主演は西島秀俊、運転手は三浦透子が演じている。この国際長編映画賞の受賞は、2009年の滝田洋二郎監督の『おくりびと』以来の快挙である。

授賞式で、濱口竜介監督は、「ここが到達点だったらいやだ。通過点だということです」とさらなる飛躍へ意欲を見せた。濱口監督の演出術について、映画評論家の蓮實氏は、「運動と静止、饒舌と沈黙、未知と既知、距離と密着、類似と差異、等の容易には解消しがたい対立に進んで身をさらす者だけが真の映画作家たりうる」と述べている。濱口氏が国際的に高い評価の対象になっているのは、その対立の核心に迫る彼の演出の大胆な繊細さによるのであろうと確証している。

## Reading

2-68

# Japan's 'Drive My Car' wins Academy Award for best international film

> Riding on a wave of critical acclaim and prizes, Ryusuke Hamaguchi's "Drive My Car" won the Academy Award for best international feature film in Los Angeles on Sunday.

During his acceptance speech, Hamaguchi thanked the members of the academy and his cast, including lead actor Hidetoshi Nishijima, in English, undeterred by an attempt by the band to interrupt his speech midway. He concluded his remarks by complimenting the driving skills of lead actress Toko Miura, who was behind the wheel of the film's signature Saab 900 as a chauffeur and confidant to the troubled theater director played by Nishijima.

2-69

"Drive My Car" is the second Japanese film to win in the best international feature film category, the only other being Yojiro Takita's "Departures," which won in 2009. However, Hamaguchi's film failed to snag a statuette in the three other categories for which it was nominated: best adapted screenplay, best director and best picture.

2-70

Based on a short story by Haruki Murakami, "Drive My Car" premiered at the Cannes Film Festival in July, where it won three awards, including best screenplay. It was also named the best picture in the non-English language category at the 79th Golden Globe Awards in January, and became the first non-English language film to win best picture honors from all three major U.S. critics groups: National Society of Film Critics, the New York Film Critics Circle and the Los Angeles Film Critics Association.

2-71

Despite the legions of critics calling "Drive My Car" a modern masterpiece — Peter Bradshaw of The Guardian described it as ascending to "a kind of grandeur" in a five-star review — the nearly 9,500 eligible academy voters were more reluctant to fully embrace a deliberately paced three-hour Japanese film about grief and loss.

best international film：最優秀国際長編映画賞
critical acclaim：批評家たちからの称賛
Ryusuke Hamaguchi：濱口竜介
Hidetoshi Nishijima：西島秀俊
undeterred：阻止された
complimenting ～：～を褒めたたえる
Toko Miura：三浦透子
behind the wheel of ～：～のハンドルを握る
signature：代表するもの
Saab 900：サーブ900ターボ《スウェーデン製乗用車》
chauffeur：お抱え運転手
confidant：相談相手
Yojiro Takita：滝田洋二郎
"Departures"：『おくりびと』
snag a statuette：小像（オスカー像）をさっと掴む
adapted screenplay：脚色賞
Haruki Murakami：村上春樹
premiered：封切られた、初公開された
named ～：～に選ばれた
legions of ～：多数の～
The Guardian：（ザ）ガーディアン《英国の新聞》
grandeur：尊厳さ、気高さ
more reluctant to ～：あまり～したがらない
embrace ～：～を受け入れる
loss：喪失

Nonetheless, the film's four Oscar nominations may further open what was once a mostly shut academy door to non-English language films, only 14 of which have ever been nominated for best picture. As Korean director Bong Joon-ho commented on receiving a best foreign language film award at the 2020 Golden Globes for his dark comedy "Parasite," "Once you overcome the one-inch tall barrier of subtitles, you will be introduced to so many more amazing films." "Parasite" proved that many academy voters had crossed that barrier by winning four Oscars, including a first-ever best picture award for an Asian film.

Bong Joon-ho：ポン・ジュノ
subtitles：字幕

2-72

Though "Drive My Car" didn't equal that achievement, its best international feature Oscar will improve its box-office prospects in Japan, if the example of "Departures" is any indication. Released in September 2008, Takita's film made a solid ¥2.8 billion after its Oscar triumph in February of the following year, bringing its total domestic earnings to over ¥6 billion.

equal that achievement：同等の成果を得る
box-office：興行収入
indication：兆候
triumph：受賞、偉業、勝利

"Drive My Car" opened in August of last year and earned a comparatively modest ¥30 million by the end of 2021. But it will now almost certainly accelerate back up the box-office rankings — and inspire more Japanese filmmakers to go even further on their Oscar journey.

modest：控えめな、ささやかな

By Mark Schilling
*The Japan Times, March 28, 2022*

## *Exercises*

### Multiple Choice

次の１～２の英文の質問に答え、３～５の英文を完成させるために、a～dの中から最も適切なものを１つ選びなさい。

**1.** What was the first Japanese entry to win best international feature film?

- **a.** Kurosawa's "Rashomon."
- **b.** Kawase's "The Tokyo Olympics."
- **c.** Miyazaki's "Spirited Away."
- **d.** Takita's "Departures."

**2.** Who is the original author of "Drive My Car?"

- **a.** Osamu Dazai.
- **b.** Yojiro Takita.
- **c.** Haruki Murakami.
- **d.** Ryusuke Hamaguchi.

**3.** Hidetoshi Nishijima's character has a career as a

- **a.** theater director.
- **b.** chauffeur.
- **c.** playwright.
- **d.** motor mechanic.

**4.** The director of "Drive My Car" praised ______________ of actress Toko Miura.

- **a.** the acting skills
- **b.** the directing skills
- **c.** the driving skills
- **d.** the speaking skills

**5.** The main themes of "Drive My Car" are

- **a.** sorrow and loss.
- **b.** joy and pride.
- **c.** sadness and happiness.
- **d.** silence and satisfaction.

## True or False

本文の内容に合致するものにＴ（True）、合致しないものにＦ（False）をつけなさい。

(　　) **1.** Almost 9,500 eligible persons voted for the film "Drive My Car."

(　　) **2.** More than 14 non-English language films have been nominated for best picture.

(　　) **3.** Takita's "Departures" was released in September 2018.

(　　) **4.** Hamaguchi's "Drive My Car" won three awards at the Cannes Film Festival.

(　　) **5.** Journalist Peter Bradshaw evaluated "Drive My Car" very highly.

## Vocabulary

次の英文は、the New York Times に掲載された *Onstage Slap Rattles Oscars 'CODA' Triumphs*『CODA 受賞前に、ステージ上での平手打ちは、オスカーを揺るがした』の記事の一部です。下の語群から最も適切な語を１つ選び、(　　) 内に記入しなさい。

In an Academy Awards ceremony where an onstage (　　　) between Will Smith and Chris Rock overshadowed the honors, "CODA" from Apple TV+ won the Oscar for best picture, becoming the first film from a streaming service to be welcomed into that rarefied Hollywood club.

The 94th Academy Awards on Sunday had a (　　　), irreverent tone from their start, with ABC and the Academy of Motion Picture Arts and Sciences laboring to prove that the Oscars could be lively and culturally (　　　). By the ceremony's end, it was certainly a night for the Hollywood ages.

An emotional Will Smith won the best actor Oscar for his performance in "King Richard" as the fiery, flawed coach and father of the tennis legends Venus and Serena Williams. Moments earlier, the ceremony had been (　　　) when Smith strode onstage from his seat and — in what at first seemed like it could be a preplanned bit — slapped Rock, who had just cracked a (　　　) about Smith's wife, Jada Pinkett Smith.

"Jada, I love you. G.I. Jane 2, can't wait," Rock said, a (　　　) to her shaved head. She revealed her alopecia diagnosis in 2018.

After the altercation, Smith returned to his seat and angrily shouted twice at Rock to "keep my wife's (　　　) out of your mouth", using an expletive that was bleeped by ABC. Rock tried to regain his composure, and a stunned audience, both in the theater and at home, tried to (　　　) out what had happened. Rock recovered enough to present the best documentary award to "Summer of Soul." But even an emotional acceptance speech by the film's director, Ahmir "Questlove" Thompson, could not hide the fact that many in attendance were rattled.

| altercation | derailed | figure | freewheeling |
|---|---|---|---|
| joke | name | reference | relevant |

Unit **26**

# ●平野歩夢　北京五輪での金メダル・ストーリー

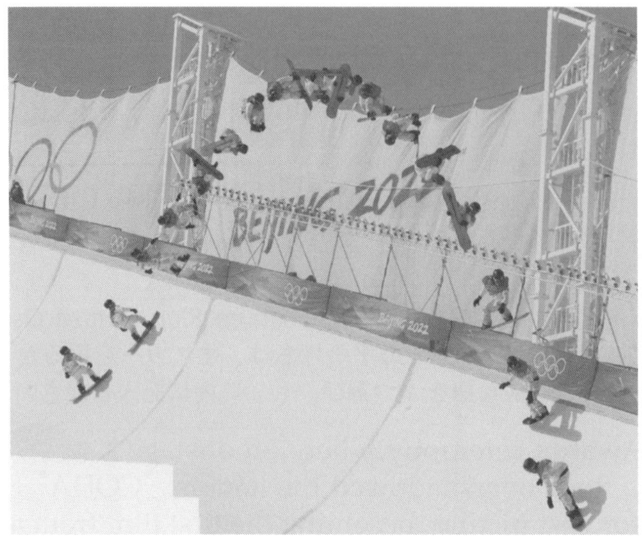


2022年北京五輪スノーボード・ハーフパイプ男子決勝で金メダルの
平野歩夢選手が演じたトリプル・コーク1440（連続写真）

The New York Times ／ Redux ／アフロ

## *Before you read*

次の１～５の英文は、フィギュア・スケートのジャンプとスピンに関する説明です。下の語群のａ～ｅから最も適切な語を１つ選び、（　　）内に記入しなさい。

**1.** a jump in skating with four turns in the air (　　　)

**2.** a jump in skating from the backward outside edge of one skate to the backward outside edge of the other, with a full turn in the air (　　　)

**3.** a jump in skating from the forward outside edge of one skate to the backward outside edge of the other, with one and a half turns in the air (　　　)

**4.** winding about a center in an enlarging or decreasing continuous circular motion turn or whirl round quickly (　　　)

**5.** turn or whirl round quickly (　　　)

**a.** axel　**b.** lutz　**c.** quadruple jump　**d.** spin　**e.** spiral

## Words and Phrases

次の１～５の語句の説明として最も近いものをａ～ｅから１つ選び、（　）内に記入しなさい。

| | | | |
|---|---|---|---|
| **1.** solidify | (　　) | **a.** | make one's position stronger |
| **2.** grab | (　　) | **b.** | be worthy of |
| **3.** daring | (　　) | **c.** | be eager to get |
| **4.** come hungry for | (　　) | **d.** | hold or grip |
| **5.** deserve | (　　) | **e.** | bold and adventurous |

## Summary

次の英文は記事の要約です。下の語群から最も適切な語を１つ選び、（　）内に記入しなさい。

2-73

The men's half-pipe final was one of the most anticipated (　　　) at the Beijing Olympics. Four Japanese, an Australian, and an American veteran all had a chance of a (　　　). Ayumu Hirano triumphed after (　　　) the first triple cork in Olympic history. The U.S. coach praised his (　　　), saying the Japanese (　　　) is easily the best in the world right now.

events　　landing　　medal　　snowboarder　　timing

2021年の東京夏季オリンピックのスケートボードに出場し、半年後、白銀の舞台に戻って来た平野歩夢選手は、スノーボード男子ハーフパイプで金メダルを獲得した。2014年のソチ大会と2018年の平昌大会で銀メダルをとり、３大会連続のメダル獲得は、冬季オリンピックの日本勢で初の快挙だった。決勝でこだわり抜いた「トリプルコーク1440（縦３回転、横４回転）」を繰り出し、96.00点の最高点をとった。ワインのコルク抜き（Corkscrew）のように、縦に３回転しながら、横に４回転（４×360°）することからこのように呼ばれる。４年前の平昌大会では、縦に１回転少ない「ダブルコーク1440」の技を決めていた。「練習を含めて一番いい滑りを、最後の最後で出せた」と充実の笑みを浮かべた。

日本は冬のオリンピックで最多となる18個のメダルを獲得した。金メダル３個、銀メダル６個、銅メダル９個で、これまで最多だった前回の平昌ピョンチャン大会の13個を５個上回る結果になった。今大会の日本代表の成績は、▼金メダル「３」 平野歩夢（スノーボード男子ハーフパイプ） 小林陵侑（スキー・ジャンプ個人ノーマルヒル） 高木美帆（スピード・スケート女子1000m） ▼銀メダル「６」 鍵山優真（フィギュア・スケート男子シングル） 小林陵侑（スキー・ジャンプ個人ラージヒル） 高木美帆（スピード・スケート女子500m・1500m） 日本（スピード・スケート女子団体パシュート）、日本（カーリング女子）、▼銅メダル「９」 宇野昌磨（フィギュア・スケート男子シングル） 堀島行真（スキー・フリースタイル男子モーグル） 森重航（スピード・スケート男子500m） 渡部暁斗（ノルディック複合個人ラージヒル） 村瀬心椛（スノー・ボード女子ビッグエア） 坂本花織（フィギュア・スケート女子シングル） 冨田せな（スノー・ボード女子ハーフパイプ） 日本（フィギュア・スケート団体） 日本（ノルディック複合団体）の18個のメダルを獲得した。

## Reading

2-74

# See How Ayumu Hirano Made Olympic History in Halfpipe to Win Gold

ZHANGJIAKOU, China — Landing a triple cork for the first time in Olympic history, Ayumu Hirano of Japan solidified his place as the world's best snowboarder with his final run at the Beijing Games, finishing atop a field of competitors that included the greatest of all time, Shaun White.

The triple cork was considered the next-level trick of these Olympics. Only Hirano had landed it in a competition earlier this winter, but he fell later during that run. No one had landed the triple cork and completed a contest run upright — until now.

2-75

Hirano is small in stature, and his triple cork was a tight ball. It consisted of three flips performed on an off-axis rotation (like a corkscrew), and Hirano did it while grabbing his board with both hands.

It was a feat of athleticism so daring that no other competitor even tried it. Hirano did it without hesitation, landing it as the opening maneuver on all three of his runs.

The men's halfpipe final at Genting Snow Park was one of the Olympics' most anticipated events. Four Japanese snowboarders had realistic chances for places on the podium, and Australia's Scotty James came hungry for a gold medal. And then there was White, the three-time gold medalist, who was making his final Olympics appearance.

2-76

Competitors made three runs in the final. Only their best score counted.

Having landed his run's premier trick comfortably and with speed, Hirano — maybe the world's smoothest rider through the transition zone between tricks — moved on to another difficult one that he lands with regularity: the Cab Double Cork 1440.

It was a twist on a familiar trick among top riders, the

Ayumu Hirano：平野歩夢

ZHANGJIAKOU：張家口

triple cork：トリプル・コーク1440《斜めの軸に縦３回転、横４回転する大技：トリプルが縦３回転、コークがらせん状に渦を巻く回転、1440は360×４で横４回転》

run：滑走、ラン

field：分野、世界

trick：トリック技

tight ball：丸まり込み

flips：フリップ《板を蹴って回転させる技》

off-axis rotation：軸外回転

maneuver：戦略

Genting Snow Park：雲頂スキー公園

anticipated：期待された

podium：表彰台

counted：重要だった

premier：最初で最高の技

comfortably：何の問題もなく

with regularity：いつものように

Cab Double Cork 1440：キャブ・ダブル・コーク1440《キャブはスイッチスタンスのフロントサイドを示す》

twist on ～：～にひねりを加えたもの

Frontside Double 1260. But Hirano did it switch, with his usual front foot in back, and added half a rotation. Few can do it.

switch：スタンスが逆向きで

2-77

Now Hirano was cruising, building momentum through his run. But none of what he had performed so far would matter if he couldn't land his last three tricks. The Frontside Double Cork 1260, common to the men's field, is another off-axis trick — midway between a spin and a flip.

cruising：落ち着いた様子で進む
building momentum：勢いをつける
matter：重要だ

"The sort of touch and timing that he has is second to none," said Mike Jankowski, the head coach of the United States freeski and snowboard teams. "He's the best in the world right now, by far, and he deserved to win, 100 percent."

second to none：誰にも負けない
by far：間違いなく
deserved to 〜：〜するのに値した
100 percent：絶対だ

2-78

White, the 35-year-old five-time Olympian who inspired many of his younger competitors, scored an 85 on his second run, good enough for fourth place and giving him hope for a storybook ending to his career.

On his third and final run, however, White attempted an ambitious ride that could put him on the medal stand one last time. But he fell on his second jump as he tried a Cab Double Cork 1440 Method, leaving him just short of his fourth Olympic medal in five tries. He took off his helmet to wave goodbye to his Olympic career.

one last time：最後にもう一度
short of 〜：〜に届かなかった
wave goodbye to 〜：〜に手を振り別れの挨拶をする

By John Branch, Weiyi Cai, Jon Huang,
Emily Rhyne, Bedel Saget, Daniel Victor,
Joe Ward, Jeremy White and Josh Williams
*The New York Times, February 11, 2022*

## *Exercises*

### Multiple Choice

次の１～５の英文を完成させるために、ａ～ｄの中から最も適切なものを１つ選びなさい。

**1.** Ayumu Hirano won a gold medal after landing

- **a.** the first double cork in Olympic history.
- **b.** the first triple cork in Olympic history.
- **c.** the highest flip in Olympic history.
- **d.** the fastest spin in Olympic history.

**2.** Hirano's winning trick consisted of

- **a.** three spins executed through an on-axis rotation.
- **b.** four flips completed with an off-axis rotation.
- **c.** double spins worked out on an on-axis rotation.
- **d.** three flips performed on an off-axis rotation.

**3.** The men's halfpipe final at Genting Snow Park was one of the Olympics'

- **a.** most awaited competitions.
- **b.** most controversial events.
- **c.** least athletic disciplines.
- **d.** least elegant battles.

**4.** Shaun White was __________ Olympian and __________ gold medalist.

- **a.** a five-time ～ four-time
- **b.** a three-time ～ three-time
- **c.** a four-time ～ four-time
- **d.** a five-time ～ three-time

**5.** While ________________, Hirano performed the triple cork.

- **a.** grabbing his board with the fingers
- **b.** grabbing his board with his hands
- **c.** holding his board with his right hand
- **d.** holding his board with his left hand

## True or False

本文の内容に合致するものにT（True）、合致しないものにF（False）をつけなさい。

(　　) **1.** The off-axis Frontside Double Cork 1260 is midway between a spin and a switch.

(　　) **2.** The winner is the competitor with the best average score over three runs.

(　　) **3.** Mike Jankowski spoke highly of Hirano's touch and timing.

(　　) **4.** No snowboarder had ever landed a triple cork in competition before.

(　　) **5.** Shaun White's helmet fell off during his second jump.

## Vocabulary

次の１～８は、「冬のスポーツをする」という意味です。日本文に合わせて（　）内に、適当な動詞を下の語群から１つ選び、必要があれば適当な形に直して記入しなさい。

**1.** 明日はスノー・ボードをやろう。
Let's (　　　　　　) snowboarding tomorrow!

**2.** 霧の中で滑っていたら、スキーがとれてしまった。
While (　　　　　　) in fog, my ski came off.

**3.** ボブスレーの名人だ。
He is good at (　　　　　　).

**4.** サンタクロースはそりに乗ると伝えられている。
Santa Claus is said to (　　　　　　) in a sleigh.

**5.** バイアスロンは、クロスカントリーと射撃で構成されている。
Biathlon consists of cross-country skiing and rifle (　　　　　　).

**6.** フィギュア・スケートが大好きだ。
She loves (　　　　　　).

**7.** ハーフパイプの練習をやる予定だ。
He is going to (　　　　　　) snowboard halfpipe.

**8.** 高校の時、アイスホッケーをよくやった。
In high school, I often (　　　　　　) ice hockey.

| bobsled | figure skate | go | play |
|---|---|---|---|
| practice | ride | shoot | ski |

ニュースメディアの英語
──演習と解説2023年度版──

検印省略

Ⓒ2023年1月31日 初版発行

編著者 高橋 優身
伊藤 典子
Richard Powell

発行者 小川 洋一郎

発行所 株式会社朝日出版社
101-0065 東京都千代田区西神田3-3-5
電話 (03) 3239-0271
FAX (03) 3239-0479
e-mail: text-e@asahipress.com
振替口座 00140-2-46008
組版・製版/信毎書籍印刷株式会社

乱丁,落丁本はお取り替えいたします
ISBN 978-4-255-15696-5 C1082

**ちょっと手ごわい、でも効果絶大!**
**最強のリスニング強化マガジン**

ENGLISH EXPRESS

音声ダウンロード付き　毎月6日発売　定価1,263円(本体1,148円+税10%)

定期購読をお申し込みの方には
本誌1号分無料ほか、特典多数。
詳しくは下記ホームページへ。

**英語が楽しく続けられる!**

重大事件から日常のおもしろネタ、
スターや著名人のインタビューなど、
CNNの多彩なニュースを
生の音声とともにお届けします。
3段階ステップアップ方式で
初めて学習する方も安心。
どなたでも楽しく続けられて
実践的な英語力が身につきます。

**資格試験の強い味方!**

ニュース英語に慣れれば、TOEIC®テストや英検の
リスニング問題も楽に聞き取れるようになります。

CNN ENGLISH EXPRESS ホームページ

英語学習に役立つコンテンツが満載!

[本誌のホームページ] https://ee.asahipress.com/
[編集部のTwitter] https://twitter.com/asahipress_ee

**朝日出版社** 〒101-0065 東京都千代田区西神田 3-3-5　TEL 03-3263-3321

GLobal ENglish Testing System

大学生向け団体受験用テスト

# GLENTS Basic

詳しくはWEBで!

グローバル英語力を測定
新時代のオンラインテスト

https://www.asahipress.com/special/glents/organization/

銀行のセミナー・研修でお使いいただいています

Point 01
**生の英語ニュースが素材**

Point 02
**場所を選ばず受験できるオンライン方式**

Point 03
**自動採点で結果をすぐに表示、国際指標 CEFR にも対応**

※画像はイメージです。

## テストを受けてくださった学生のみなさまの反応

◇生の英語でのテストは非常に優位性があると思いました。

◇動画問題があるのが面白い!

◇将来海外に行くときに直接役立つと感じました。

◇音声を聞くことができる回数が1回のみだったので、真の「聞いて理解する力」を試されていると思いました。

◇多様な生の英語に慣れておく必要性を感じる良い経験となりました。

### これからの大学生に求められる英語とは

企業が求める英語力はどんどん変化しています。これからの社会人は、違う文化を持つ人々と英語でしっかりコミュニケーションを取る必要があり、異文化に対する知識・理解を増やす必要があります。ですから、それらを身につけるために生の英語=CNN GLENTS Basicで英語力を測り、CNNをはじめ様々なメディアで勉強することは非常に効果の高い学習法だと感じていますし、お勧めします。

**鈴木武生氏**
東京大学大学院総合文化研究科修了(言語情報科学専攻)。専門は英語、中国語、日本語の意味論。1991 年にアジアユーロ言語研究所を設立。企業向けスキル研修、翻訳サービスなどを手掛ける。

受験料:大学生 1 人あたり 2,200 円(税込)　受験料は、受けていただく学生の人数によってご相談させていただきます。

株式会社 朝日出版社「CNN GLENTS」事務局　☎0120-181-202　✉glents_support@asahipress.com

® & © Cable News Network A WarnerMedia Company. All Rights Reserved.

# 生きた英語でリスニング!

1本30秒だから、聞きやすい!

## CNN ニュース・リスニング

2022［春夏］

電子書籍版付き
ダウンロード方式で提供

［30秒×3回聞き］方式で
世界標準の英語がだれでも聞き取れる!

- 羽生結弦、「氷上の王子」の座はゆずらない
- オックスフォード英語辞典にKカルチャー旋風
- 「母語」と「外国語」を犬も聞き分けている!…など

MP3音声・電子書籍版付き
（ダウンロード方式）
A5判 定価1100円（税込）

初級者からのニュース・リスニング

## CNN Student News

2022 夏秋

音声アプリ+動画で、どんどん聞き取れる!

- レベル別に2種類の速度の音声を収録
- ニュース動画を字幕あり/なしで視聴できる

MP3・電子書籍版・
動画付き［オンライン提供］
A5判 定価1,320円（税込）

朝日出版社 〒101-0065 東京都千代田区西神田 3-3-5 TEL 03-3263-3321

**累計50万部のベストセラー辞典**
**待望の改訂新版!**

# 最新 日米口語辞典 [決定版]

エドワード・G・サイデンステッカー＋
松本道弘＝共編

定価5,280円（税込）
A5判変型（196mm×130mm）函入り　1312ページ

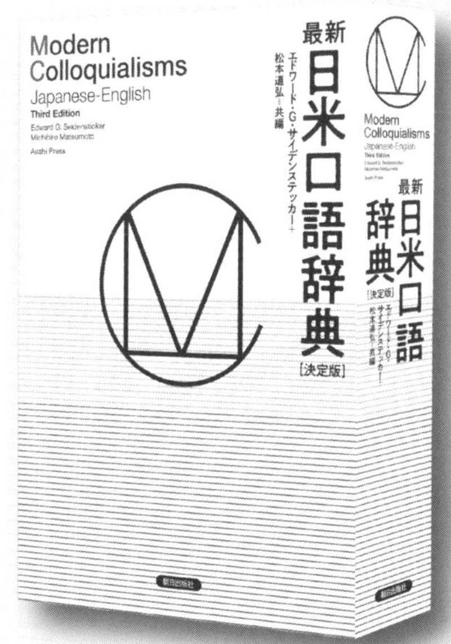


◉表現の羅列ではなく、解説を読んで楽しめる辞典
◉硬い辞書訳から脱却し、日常的な口語表現を採用
◉品詞にこだわらず、日本語のニュアンスを最もよく伝える表現を採用
◉ニュアンスや使い分けを詳しく説明
◉「忖度する」「歩きスマホ」「無茶振り」など、今時の言葉を多数増補

朝日出版社　〒101-0065 東京都千代田区西神田 3-3-5　TEL 03-3263-3321